THAT LAND OF EXILES
SCOTS IN AUSTRALIA

'First Gathering of the Bendigo Caledonian Society, Jan. 2, 1860', by
George Lacy. *By permission of the National Library of Australia.*

THAT
LAND OF EXILES

SCOTS · IN · AUSTRALIA

HER MAJESTY'S STATIONERY OFFICE
EDINBURGH
1988

British Library Cataloguing in Publication data
That land of exiles: Scots in Australia,
  1. Australia. Society. Role of Scots 1788-1988
  I. Richards, Eric
  305.8'9163   ISBN 0 11 493425 8

Note: The title of the book, 'That Land of Exiles', is taken from a letter of Lachlan Macquarie, dated 22 April 1809, to his friend, Charles Forbes, in which he writes: 'When I last wrote to you I thought I should by this time have been half way on my passage to Botany Bay . . . that Land of Exiles'.

Cover illustration: 'First Gathering of the Bendigo Caledonian Society, Jan. 2, 1860', by George Lacy.
By permission of the National Library of Australia.

Colour illustrations: With the exception of the frontispiece and the portrait miniatures on page 19, the colour illustrations in the book are by Sophia Campbell (1777-1833), wife of Robert Campbell, the pioneer merchant and pastoralist who founded Duntroon in 1825, and her daughter-in-law, Marrianne Campbell (1827-1903). They are reproduced by kind permission of Mrs J. Campbell, Mrs J. H. P. Curtis and Mrs M. A. Norman.

ISBN 0 11 493425 8

CONTENTS

ACKNOWLEDGEMENTS

The Trustees of the National Library of Scotland wish to express their gratitude to owners, private and institutional, who have provided photographs for reproduction in the publication: Aberdeen Art Gallery and Museums; Aberdeen University Library; Australian Overseas Information Service, London; Ben Line Group; British Museum (Natural History); Martin J. Buckley, Esq., Goonelabah, New South Wales; Mrs J. Campbell, Mrs J. H. P. Curtis and Mrs M. A. Norman; City of Edinburgh Museums and Art Galleries; Croom Helm Ltd, Publishers; Franklin Watts, Publishers; James G. Fisher, Esq.; Mary MacKillop Research Centre, Sydney; Mitchell Library, State Library of New South Wales; National Library of Australia; National Portrait Gallery; New South Wales Government Printing Office; Oxford University Press, Melbourne; Royal Geographical Society of Australasia (South Australia Branch), Adelaide; Royal Historical Society of Victoria, Melbourne; Tasmanian Museum and Art Gallery.

INTRODUCTION

The idea of this publication, and its associated exhibition, to mark the occasion of the Australian Bicentennial, arose out of a conversation between Dr Ian Donnachie of the Open University in Scotland, Dr Ian Duffield of the University of Edinburgh, and Dr Ann Matheson of the National Library of Scotland, at the Colloquium on Australian and New Zealand Studies arranged by the British Library in London from 7 to 9 February 1984.

The National Library is delighted to be associated with the Bicentennial celebrations, and to have this opportunity to bring before the public the varied historical evidence of the strong and lasting links between Scotland and Australia. In recent years, the tradition of Scots making their way to Australia in search of opportunity has been enhanced by the growth of a reciprocal interest in Scotland on the part of the Australian business community. We are delighted to be able to reflect this two-way association in our publication by including essays by both Australian and Scottish scholars.

We are grateful to Professor Eric Richards of Flinders University, South Australia, Dr Ian Donnachie of the Open University in Scotland, and Dr Adrian Graves of the University of Edinburgh, for contributing chapters to the volume. Thanks are also due to Mrs Alexia Howe, Assistant Keeper in the Department of Printed Books, who prepared the rest of the volume, and the exhibition; and to the many, both in Scotland and in Australia, who have assisted us in a variety of ways, and have thus helped to make the Bicentennial an occasion to remember.

E. F. D. ROBERTS
Librarian
April 1988

The Butts of Ben Lomond, Tasmania.

SCOTTISH AUSTRALIA 1788-1914

Scotch Colonies in the Outback

The Scottish colonization of Australia began in the convict age but reached its greatest impact in the decades of gold in the mid-19th century. It ran parallel with the influx of peoples from the rest of the British Isles, from Germany and, later, elsewhere. Yet there were moments in the evolution of the Australian colonies when the Scots seemed to predominate, even to the point of giving the southern continent a distinctively Caledonian complexion. When the great pioneering grazier-squatter from Argyll, Niel Black, first arrived at Port Phillip in 1839, he exclaimed that it was 'a Scotch colony' and that 'two thirds of the inhabitants are Scotch'. On the gold fields in the 1850s each new rush had its Highland camp and in the evenings the sound of bagpipes was carried over the broken landscape. There were entire districts in several Australian colonies in which Scottish settlers preponderated, sometimes for more than a generation.

Australia, therefore, was part of the wider Scottish empire. In company with other parts of the world newly invaded by Europeans, Australia acknowledged the Scottish presence. Scottish origins are often still evoked for sentimental and political effect. Recent prime ministers and political leaders have invoked, even traded upon, their Scottish roots, and often to the disadvantage of their non-Scottish ancestors. There are symbols of Scotland across the continent, in place-names, Scots churches, statues of Robert Burns, Caledonian societies, Scotch colleges, and in endless professional bodies glorying in Scottish names, notably among lawyers, doctors and engineers. Many modern Australians would acknowledge also the prevailing influence of Scottish culture and thought. For instance, the dominant ideology of *laissez-faire* capitalism sprang in part from Adam Smith and the philosophers of the Scottish Enlightenment. No one would deny the widespread influence of Scottish Calvinism in colonial Australia, often pitted against Irish Catholicism and the primitive anarchies of the outback. Scottish habits of thought brought powerful instruments of social control to many of the new communities created in colonial Australia.

Many societies were established by Scottish immigrants in the new colonies in a conscious effort to foster pride in Scots origins. One such was the Scotch Association which first met in Geelong in July 1853. Its purpose was 'the moral and social elevation of its members, and performance of acts of benevolence towards Scottish people in this colony'. One of its supporters said that Scotland, 'this land of mountain and flood', was at the head of all nations in agricultural science and education and 'sends out the greatest amount of intellect and worth in other lands; she gives most and gets least'. Too many Scots, he said, were ashamed of their country and 'tried to be English'. To resist such unthinking absorption, and to proclaim the virtues of the Scots immigrants, was a recurrent theme in the proliferation of these émigré societies.

In their search for a continued identity in Australia, the Scots inevitably sought to emphasize the distinctiveness of their impact on the new colonies. Yet, in the process, it was easy to lose sight of the similarities between the Scots and the

Scots' Church, Melbourne. *Australasian Sketcher,* 20 March 1875.

other component elements in the colonization of Australia. Most Scottish immigrants, indeed, dispersed into the general population, blending into the emergent Australian people. Few permanent, identifiable, Scottish concentrations survived for much more than a single generation; their original distinctiveness was swiftly diluted by the processes of assimilation. Nor were the Scots necessarily strikingly different, in many characteristics, from other immigrants. Often they had departed from similar economic conditions, similar levels of literacy, a similar religious and cultural context, and similar family origins.

The general stereotype of the immigrant Scot was itself deceptive. Many Scots were not Presbyterian. Some of the most influential Australian Scots were opposed to the political economy derived from the philosophers of Edinburgh and Glasgow. The greatest opponent of free trade in late 19th–century Australia was David Syme (1827-1908), rebellious son of a North Berwick manse and one-time gold-digger. Syme became an immensely influential editor of the Melbourne *Age,* and the most effective advocate of protectionism for Australian producers. It is, indeed, difficult to disentangle the specifically Scottish contribution to Australian life, and even more to demonstrate that it was disproportionately formative. Nor were all Scottish influences necessarily positive or welcome: for instance, the legacy of Presbyterians which nourished 'wowserism' (an Australian term referring to killjoys or Puritans) in colonial life, remains a tarnished memory even today.

The Scots in Australia existed in remarkable diversity which mocks the stereotype that, sometimes, the Scots themselves cultivated. Rural and urban, Highland and Lowland, opulent and destitute, rising and declining, adventurous and desperate, ignorant and educated, mobile and static — their diversity was a full mirror of Scottish society in the 19th century. But this is not to say that it was a formless variety; there were, indeed, identifiable uniformities in the flows of people and influences between Scotland and Australia. There emerged an important complementarity between the two societies. Links were established and a confidence created, by which the Scots helped colonize Australia. This was particularly true of commercial connexions and capital exports. But, most of all, the emigration of Scots to Australia reflected the shifting, indeed dynamic, evolution of Scotland itself during the many decades in which Australia improvised a series of new and experimental societies on the opposite side of the globe.

Australian Scots

Scotland was generous, even prodigal, with its people in the 19th century. In the great age of international migration the Scots were, after the Irish, the most migratory people in Europe. This was reflected in their demographic contribution to Australia. Such was the scale of Irish and Scottish immigration that Australian historians have found it necessary to employ the phrase 'Anglo-Celtic' to describe the main mixture of the pre-1945 population.

The exact Scottish component of the Australian population is surprisingly difficult to measure. Emigrants in the 19th-century world of liberal free trade were subject to less surveillance than those of a later age. Bureaucracies were less developed and there were fewer impediments to movement. Consequently, private passenger movements and self-financing migrations were frequently unrecorded in shipping and port statistics. Much more is known about the migrants who travelled by government assistance schemes such as the bounty migrants of the 1830s, and the many others who followed. The Australian colonial censuses are also helpful because they record the proportions of the population born outside Australia.

In the years 1853 to 1880, Scots accounted for about 10 per cent of all British emigrants to all destinations. But they were 13 per cent of those destined for Australasia, which suggests that they made disproportionate use of assisted passages. Nevertheless, far more Scots went to England and North America than to Australia. Official records indicate that 138,036 Scots arrived in Australasia in these years. They were mainly described as domestic servants and general

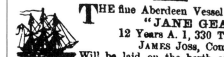
Advertisement for the *Jane Geary,* sailing from Aberdeen to Port Phillip, *Aberdeen Journal,* 14 July 1852. *By permission of Aberdeen University Library.*

labourers and reached Australia with the assistance of colonial governments. Males outnumbered females by almost three to two. The Scots evidently supplied a general range of proletarian skills for the benefit of Australian development. This point is often forgotten amid so many stories of outstanding Scottish success in the commercial and professional life of Australia. In fact, Scotland provided a disproportion of the basic bone and sinew of the colonization of the continent.

Several of the colonies, notably Victoria and South Australia, regarded the Scots as the best migrants. They instructed their emigration agents to recruit more vigorously in Scotland, and some of them were at work in the remotest districts as early as 1837. Scots immigrants were favoured because of their education, their frugality, their malleability and their energy. Just as important, however, was the fact that the Scots were regarded as counterweight to the increasingly Irish, and, therefore, increasingly Catholic, character of the colonial population of Australia. Colonial authorities set out to recruit Scots rather than the Irish, often at considerable extra expense.

Colonial labour requirements fluctuated as sharply as those in the British Isles, and they were at their most extreme in the great gold rushes of the 1850s. Similarly, the propensity to emigrate from Scotland varied markedly with the harvest and the trade cycle. There were times (discussed *infra*) when colonial emigration agencies probed deep into the remotest districts of Scotland seeking transcontinental migrants among people set in the most immobile peasant populations in the British Isles, notably those in the Outer Hebrides and the North-West Highlands. Active discrimination of this sort caused some of the most marginal elements in Victorian Scotland, such as the St Kilda crofters and the Shetland fishermen, to undertake the enormous voyage to the other side of the planet. Australia became home to some of the outcasts of the Scottish Highlands during its most difficult decades of adjustment to industrialization. At other times later in the 19th century, Australia recruited from the more migration-conscious and mobile elements in the industrial towns and cities of Lowland Scotland. Throughout the century, Highland and Lowland Scotland was regarded as a happy hunting ground for colonial emigration agents.

Yet, in the light of these special efforts to favour Scottish immigration, the resulting composition of the Australian population was not as Scottish as might be expected. Despite their greater propensity to emigrate, the Scots represented in the 19th century about 15 per cent of Australian immigration. Sometimes, it was higher: of the population of Port Phillip in 1846, Scots were 17 per cent of the immigrants.

	English	Scottish	Irish	Welsh	German	Scandinavian	Other European
NSW	52.2	13.0	26.3	1.8	3.3	1.6	1.8
Victoria	49.1	15.7	26.5	1.5	3.3	1.5	2.4
Queensland	45.5	13.5	26.1	1.3	9.1	3.1	1.4
S. Australia	58.2	11.0	18.5	1.8	9.0	1.2	1.3
W. Australia (1901)	54.0	11.3	21.0	1.7	3.2	3.1	5.7
Tasmania	60.0	13.5	20.0	1.2	3.3	1.2	0.8
	53.0	13.0	23.0	1.5	5.2	1.9	2.4

Adelaide, South Australia. *Illustrated London News*, 24 August 1850.

These figures show that the Scots were somewhat, though not dramatically, over-represented in the Australian population, rather more than their share of the British population would have suggested. Although Scots settled in all the colonies, there were slightly greater concentrations in Victoria and Queensland, perhaps because these colonies were settled after the main waves of convict imports had passed.

The censuses of 1891 registered the relative proportions of overseas-born within the Australian populations (see Table on page 12). In 1891, New Zealand had a substantially higher Scottish proportion of overseas-born than any of the Australian colonies.

There were, it is true, greater concentrations of Scots within some of the colonies, for example at Mount Gambier in South Australia, in the Western District of Victoria, in parts of the gold fields, and in the New England district of New South Wales. But none of these became permanent enclaves, nor exclusively Scottish settlements. Nor were later transfusions of Scottish emigrants able to sustain the earlier levels of Scottish-ness, inevitably so as the Australian-born component of the population rose inexorably. Chain-migration from Scotland was considerable in the late 19th century but could not resist the tide of assimilation. In 1971, Scots-born residents of Australia were 1.6 per cent of the total population, and 6.2 per cent of all foreign-born in the country.

The Scots were, therefore, overtaken by non-British immigrants in this century. Even though substantial numbers continued to arrive after 1945, in terms of their influence on Australia, the Scots were pre-eminently a 19th-century emigrant nation.

The Emigrant Nation

The Australian Scots were part of a much longer tradition of Scottish mobility that stretched back into the 17th century. Scots had been migrating to Ulster, to Europe and to England, apparently in rising numbers, for many decades long before Australia had even been mapped. It is also likely that the rate of internal mobility had accelerated in the last decades of the 18th century. There were people dislodged from agriculture and rural industries, people drawn magnetically to the industrial growth of central Scotland, people looking for new paths to economic security and social advance. This greater mobility was set in a vital context of population growth, a well-established phenomenon by 1780. Already, of course, Scots had been flooding across the Atlantic, but these migrations were not simply an expression of a generalized mobility. Until the late 18th century, a high proportion were migrations from very specific locations in the Western Highlands and Islands, usually in communal or family formation, often directed to particular destinations, for example, to North Carolina before the War of Independence, to Cape Breton Island and Nova Scotia afterwards. Emigration from the Lowlands, numerically, tended to be dominated by young single people, often skilled and urban in background. On the face of things, the Lowlanders were more opportunistic and mobile than their Highland countryfolk. Two broad distinctions in Scottish emigration, though imperfect in many respects and subject to a multitude of exceptions, helped to give a simple pattern to a great movement of people which is, otherwise, confusingly kaleidoscopic in character.

In general terms, Scottish emigration to the Antipodes was an extension and a variant of the transatlantic pattern. The same general stimuli were at work, producing similar flows of Scottish migration. Except for a few years (1853-54, 1860-64, 1875-77), however, it was considerably smaller than the Atlantic outflows. Moreover, the much greater expense and distance of Australian migration created special problems and biases in the recruitment of Scots for Australia. Much of early Australian history was marked by a series of expedients and improvisations designed to overcome what a modern historian, Geoffrey Blainey, has labelled 'the tyranny of distance'. Various mechanisms were invented to induce immigration. Convictism itself was one solution; so were the emerging schemes for subsidising passages out of colonial revenues, particularly from land sales. Yet, while these mechanisms were being developed, Australia was in the throes of change, as much as Scotland itself. Australia, by the 1830s, was emerging out of its convict origins, as from a chrysalis. But the most overwhelming transformation of colonial Australia was wrought by gold.

Gold revolutionized immigration. The sensational discoveries in Victoria and New South Wales whipped up extraordinary rushes within a few weeks. The invasion of the gold fields was under way by August 1851. Gold was immensely disruptive to all aspects of colonial life. The population of Victoria (which had become a separate colony based on Port Phillip in 1850) increased from 76,000 in 1850 to 538,000 within ten years. For Scots and others, the gold rushes immediately invested Australia with a glamour and an attraction which, for a decade or more, transcended the great problem of distance.

Both before and after the gold rushes, the normal relations between Australia and its migrant donors were more prosaic and, indeed, more institutional and formally organized. The earlier preponderance of Highland immigrants tended to diminish in proportion to southern Scots. This reflected the continuing industrialization of Scotland and the mobility of its urban people. Moreover, despite so much emigration, Scotland's population continued to increase rapidly throughout the 19th century — from 1.6 million in 1801 to 4.47 million in 1901. It was an immigrant-receiving country, too: 7.2 per cent of the Scottish population

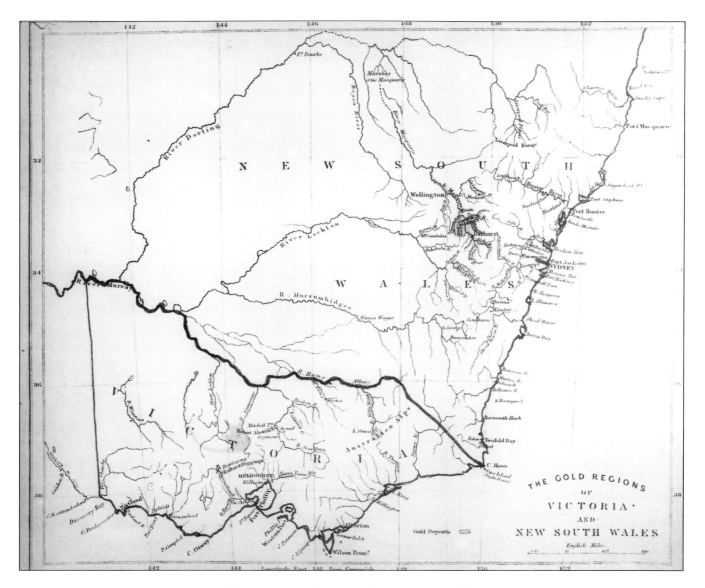

Map of the gold regions of Victoria and New South Wales, from David
Mackenzie. *The Gold Digger*. London, 1855.

'Australian Gold Diggings', by Edwin Stocqueler. *By permission of the National Library of Australia.*

in 1851 had been born in Ireland, and some of these re-emigrated to Australia. Between 1861 and 1939 Scotland lost 44 per cent of its natural increase to net emigration.

The relationship between Scotland and Australia was, therefore, between two countries in the process of rapid transformation. Parts of Scotland were in the vanguard of the Industrial Revolution, pioneering new forms of industry and productivity, creating new urban communities, recreating new commercial nexuses with Europe, America and Asia from the end of the 18th century. The intellectual vibrancy of Scotland was mirrored in its cultural exports, in its education, in its literary output, its commercial and professional acumen, its theological disputation, and was often embodied in its migrants. From the non-industrial quarters of Scotland departed other types of migrants: farmers, agricultural labourers, clan chiefs, crofters, cottars, fishermen, and rural domestic servants. Some of these were substantial capitalists in search of better returns on their capital, but some wanted to escape from poor agricultural prices, some to avoid rural redundancy, some to release themselves from a system in which inheritance was blocked by primogeniture and too many siblings. Some of them sought to escape from overpopulation, from overbearing landlords, factors and tacksmen; some were the victims of evictions; and some sought liberation from stark poverty.

Australia, concurrently, was being metamorphosed from its convict origins and functions into a new civil society, an outpost of civilization rather than a penal dumping ground. Colonization was hungry for labour, skilled and unskilled, for men and women to develop the productive base of the colonial economies. These demands became the more voracious when export staples were discovered: wool pre-eminently, then wheat, copper, sugar, coal and gold, and cattle by the end of the century. But the demands for labour became rapidly differentiated and diversified: the organization of the colonies required legions of administrators and managers, teachers and preachers, and the emergent professional and service sectors of the economy required people trained beyond the basic capacities of unskilled migrants. Before Australia was able to educate its own recruits, it imported great numbers of more highly qualified immigrants. Scotland was one of the best sources, especially for the managerial and professional ranks. The process of colonization also required endless injections of capital, and this again came from abroad in advance of the colonies' own capacity to generate an indigenous supply. Australia in the 19th century was one of the great capital-importing regions of the *Pax Britannica*. Scotland, again, was disproportionately attuned to these needs. In the late 19th century, an especially close connexion grew up between the Scottish suppliers of capital and the developers of Australian resources. Scots emerged strongly in the world of Antipodean banking and finance.

Consequently, while drawing broadly on Scottish human and capital resources, Australia was able to tap particular reservoirs and flows of Scottish life and culture. The resultant migrations, across more than 12,000 miles of ocean to Sydney, Melbourne and Adelaide, reflected the changing disposition of Scotland and its regions as much as the shifting circumstances of the Great Southern Continent. By the end of the 19th century, the pattern had altered. While Scotland became a mature and urban society, Australia itself had entered the infant, somewhat precarious, phases of industrialization. The cities grew very rapidly. Thus, between 1860 and 1914, despite its 'colonial' structure and its primary-producing export industries, Australia became one of the most urbanized countries in the world, exceeding, for instance, the United States in this regard. The capital cities —Adelaide, Brisbane, Hobart, Melbourne, Perth and Sydney— increasingly dominated their hinterlands and absorbed their populations.

For the Scots and other British emigrants, the consequence was simple: more and more, they were emigrating from an urban place in their homeland to an urban centre in Australia. Moreover, they were leaving Scotland at a time when Scottish living standards were improving at an

Port Melbourne.

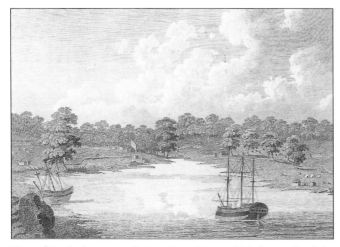

View of the Settlement on Sydney Cove, August 1788, from a sketch by
John Hunter.

unprecedented rate. By the end of the 19th century, emigration from Scotland to Australia had become an urban experience at both ends of the nexus.

Convicts and Officers

Among Australian historians, there is a lingering debate about the reasons why Britain began a settlement at Botany Bay in 1788. To its obvious penal colony function is sometimes added, by rival schools of thought, the notion that it was a strategic ploy to pre-empt other imperial powers in the Pacific. This may or may not have been complemented by a veiled purpose of securing commercial advantages in the East India trade. While the controversy continues to erupt sporadically, it is clear that Scots were associated with each of the three functions of early Australia. They were also instrumental in the transformation of New South Wales and Van Diemen's Land from the convict colony in 1788 into a civil society by the 1820s.

Convicts arrived at Botany Bay in 1788 and were introduced into Van Diemen's Land (later Tasmania) from 1803. Moreton Bay (in present-day Queensland) received convicts as early as 1829 and free settlers in 1842, but its growth was very slow. South Australia chose not to take part in the transportation system, but the rest of the continent eventually absorbed about 150,000 convicts before the system was abolished in the mid century. Western Australia, desperate for any kind of labour, was in 1868 the last to abandon the importation of convicts.

There were relatively few Scots among the convicts arriving in Australia. They were less than 3 per cent of the total and, therefore, much under-represented in the criminal origins of Australia. In the first dozen years of the Botany Bay colony, only 70 Scots were received, and by 1823 the total had increased only to 855. In *per capita* terms, the English were four times more numerous. In part, the shortfall in Scottish numbers was accounted for by differences between Scots and English law. The Scots system was more selective, and

Portrait miniatures of Sophia and Robert Campbell, by an unknown
artist.

St Phillip's Church, Sydney, *c.* 1816, by Sophia Campbell.

Aboriginal mother and child, from a sketch by John Hunter.

reserved its extreme punishments for its worst offenders and recidivists. Looking back over half a century of Scottish transportation, Archibald Alison stated that the Scots transported were 'persons only who were deemed irreclaimable in this country', people who had committed extremely grave offences, or who had been convicted many times over. They were 'a class of repeatedly convicted and hardened offenders'.

The reputation of this relatively small number of Scots convicts echoed these origins. They were the most feared and dangerous of the convict population. The ordinary petty offenders who swelled the English, Welsh and Irish numbers were missing in the Scottish criminal exports. Of the convicts it was said 'the most base and clever are the Scotch', who were 'beyond all question, the worst who arrive'. In general, the Scots arrived at Botany Bay after time spent in the hulks at Portsmouth or Woolwich, and their crimes were more serious than the average. Most of them, in reality, were burglars or housebreakers, usually committed after a trial in Edinburgh or Glasgow which took account of previous convictions. Among the female convicts was a larger than average proportion of prostitutes who had served a long career. Some leavening of this mass of ordinary Scottish criminality was provided by the most famous of the Scots convict immigrants – the 'Scottish Martyrs' of 1793-94. These were men caught in the trials for sedition during the French Wars and punished as a result of their struggle for democracy and revolution. In Australia these men – who included Thomas Muir and Fyshe Palmer – were treated relatively well, and probably left less mark on Australian political culture than other political exiles, notably their Irish counterparts. Another well-known Scottish convict was Margaret McKinnon from Skye, who had been transported with the First Fleet for 'having set fire to her neighbour's house in a fit of jealousy'. A Gaelic-speaker herself, she eventually married Phillip Shoeffer, a German, who was thought to be the first free immigrant to Australia, and the first to obtain a land grant in the colony. More generally, however, Scottish convicts in Australia reflected the growth of urban crime in Scotland, and the character of the Scottish legal system.

Convictism naturally raised questions of penology and prison administration. In the pre-1788 debate about transportation to New South Wales, the convict scheme had been noisily opposed in Scotland by Lord Gardenstone. He regarded the whole idea as a shockingly expensive method of dealing with the problem of crime: it was 'the most absurd, prodigal and impractical vision that ever intoxicated the mind of man'. But these opinions did not prevail in the face of the more powerful English lobby, which argued that the nation was confronted with a massive breakdown of law and order, demanding drastic solutions.

The administration of the convict colony, which, within three decades, began to evolve into a recognisably civilized community, created new opportunities for the exercise of Scottish talents. At the very top was Captain John Hunter (born in Leith and educated briefly at Aberdeen University), who arrived with the First Fleet in January 1788, and became the second Governor of the Colony. In October 1788, he had been sent back to the Cape of Good Hope to collect desperately needed provisions for the failing convict settlement. His mission succeeded, and Hunter became Governor on his return from London in September 1794. Now aged 57, he was under instructions to re-assert imperial policy in the colony and to correct abuses such as the illicit import of spirituous liquor. Hunter faced increasing difficulties among both the convicts and the officer corps, but he was successful in promoting the further exploration of the southern continent. He also fostered agriculture and mining and witnessed the rise of the population of the colony to 5,000 by the time he left the colony in 1800. Already there was, from the ranks of the officers and emancipated convicts, the beginning of free settlement. Hunter was recalled to London amid growing controversy about the structure of authority in the colony.

The most illustrious of all colonial administrators was Lachlan Macquarie (1762-1824), who replaced the notorious Bligh to re-establish firm control, practical administration and commercial reforms. Governor Macquarie, indeed, was credited with the achievement of making New South Wales a humane civilian society in the critical years between 1810 and 1820, during which time a further 18,500 convicts arrived in the colony. 'Macquarie was the last governor able to impose a personal stamp on the colony.' During his administration, the colony broke out of its original geographical restraints, crossed the Blue Mountains, and opened the vigorous development of free enterprise beyond the direct control of the government sector. This was the great transition in early colonial Australia, and Macquarie possessed a vision of progress which became manifest in the development of a free society, sometimes in advance of the expectations and consent of London and the Colonial Office.

Macquarie was a fine exemplar of a certain Scottish background. Commander of the 73rd Regiment of

Scene near the Darling, 11 July 1835, by Thomas Livingston Mitchell.

Highlanders, he represented the stratum of mobile regimental Highlanders from the higher echelons of northern life. He was the son of a factor on the isle of Ulva, where he claimed some chieftainly connexions. He was one of many who saw far better opportunities in military service with the British crown than in the insular world of the West Highlands. He is said to have taken army service and command in the East to avoid financial ruin at home.

As Governor, Macquarie was a humanitarian who conceived that he had a duty to the whole population of the colony, 'be they bond or free, black or white'. Opponents in London eventually began to undermine his progressive policies, re-asserting the deterrent function of the colony, and emphasizing the founding principle of its formation, that it be self-sufficient. After twelve years Macquarie could say, 'I found New South Wales a jail and left it a colony'. By October 1821, the population had increased to nearly 30,000, and it was plainly outgrowing its original function.

Macquarie was succeeded by another Scot, but one of a different stamp. Sir Thomas Brisbane, Governor of New

South Wales from 1821 to 1825, was also a career officer, but one who had advanced from a relatively secure background in landed society in Lowland Ayrshire. Beneath Brisbane and his successors were other layers of Scots administrators at all levels. The Scots were advantaged by their prominence in military life, which gave them secure career paths. The path to Australia usually began in army service, then time in India, and then a natural progression into the officer corps in New South Wales. This could then be followed by land grants in the colony, and by some form of family settlement. Consequently, there was a considerable Highland element in the early decades, which helped to establish secure nexuses, and facilitated more broadly-based civilian immigration in the 1820s and thereafter.

Much of the security and defence of the nascent colony in Australia in its first decade was vested in the hands of battle-hardened Scots units, notably the 73rd Highlanders, the Perthshires, and the 2nd Battalion of the Black Watch. Since there was, in the event, little external threat (even during the French Wars), and relatively slight difficulties internally from the Aborigines, the energy of the troops was employed to extend the colonial infrastructure, most notably in the great road and urban construction programme under Macquarie.

One Scot exerted a vital role in the theory and practice of penology in early Australia, and provided a link between some of the more practical notions of the Scottish Enlightenment and the development of intellectual life in Australia. In some sense, the work of Captain Alexander Maconochie (1787-1860) was Scotland's compensation for dispatching its worst criminals to Australia. Maconochie was responsible for the eventual reform of the convict transportation system. He was the orphaned son of a Scottish land agent, who first made his way in the world in the navy; subsequently, he became the first Professor of Geography at University College, London, in 1833. Four years later, he visited Port Phillip and reported on the penal system in Australia for the Society for the Improvement of Prison Discipline. It is not surprising that Australia should have generated new thinking in the arena of convict discipline and rehabilitation — the colony was a working social laboratory. Maconochie advocated a work system for prisoners with the intention of giving them incentives for early release by allowing them to demonstrate their own personal reform. In 1839, Maconochie was appointed to the command of the penal colony in Norfolk Island — a notorious hell-hole. There he practised his highly controversial theories which were, inevitably, dogged by opposition throughout his career in penal administration. In the long run, however, Maconochie exerted a permanent influence on penological ideas, especially his notion of 'the indeterminate sentence'. He was the most advanced and humanitarian penologist of his day and his name is still honoured in the literature.

Scots and the Genesis of Australian Commerce

Australia's colonial history was dominated by three great themes, which shifted in their significance during the first half century of European settlement: relations with the native peoples of the continent; the role of the convict system; and the emergence of the private sector. For most of the time, the Aboriginal question was left in the shadows, while disease and grotesque inter-racial violence took their toll, sometimes leaving Scots settlers with a stained reputation. The greater challenge seemed to be the conversion of the penal colony towards a self-sufficient civil society. The task required capital, enterprise and free immigration. At the beginning, it required also a vision, and a response to the possibilities of the continent. Certain types of Scots were able to supply Australian requirements, possibly beyond their numerical proportions.

The economic exploration of the new continent needed as much daring and initiative as its geographical exploration. In the first faltering steps of Australian commerce, one man, a Scot, stood out. Robert Campbell's career (1769-1846) exemplified several vital connexions in the genesis of Australian overseas trade. In particular, his own commercial progress demonstrated the place of India as a staging post in Antipodean colonization. Indeed, Campbell's trading

Aborigine throwing a spear.

the first products to demonstrate that Australia could develop a two-way economic relationship with the rest of the British world. It was the key to its escape from its role as a penitentiary.

There were, however, large impediments facing Campbell's enterprise. He was opposed by powerful interests, most notably those of the East India Company, which held a vice-like control on Eastern trade. Campbell also led conscious efforts to liberate colonial trade from the clutches of the ruling officer corps, which dominated the import trade of the colony. By 1805, Campbell was already exporting skins directly to London in defiance of the East India Company, and for another decade he fought for the extension of free trade to Australia. This was eventually capped with success in 1815, when Sydney was at last declared a free port. In 1819, having made good profits in government contracts to import livestock from India, Campbell helped to organize the first savings bank in Australia. Campbell became a wealthy pastoralist and a great philanthropist in the emerging civil society. Most of all, he had brought to Australia the scarce resources of capital and mercantile expertise. These enabled the infant economy to slot into the continuously expanding network of Asian trade, which was, in turn, connected beyond to Europe and America. In this way, he set the foundations of the new colonial economy, the *sine qua non* of Macquarie's vision of a civil society.

Alexander Berry (1781-1873) followed a commercial path with similar associations, bearing similar talents to Australia. Son of a tenant farmer in Fife, he had discovered that there was little chance to make a career in Lowland agriculture. He was like many other Scots who, with inheritance blocked by too many children, failed speculations or poor health, turned to Australia for better opportunities: the father of the novelist, Catherine Helen Spence, lost most of his money on the wheat exchanges in 1839, and departed for South Australia to recover his fortunes. Alexander Berry, however, had received a good education at the universities of St Andrews and Edinburgh and, blessed with wide horizons, he became the very model

initiatives in New South Wales were, in essence, an offshoot of his involvement in the East India trade. His operations in early Sydney were a natural extension of the Campbell family's enterprise involved in a Scottish trade between Glasgow and Calcutta.

Campbell arrived in New South Wales in 1798 to reconnoitre its trading possibilities, and to establish a branch of Campbell, Clarke and Company, merchants trading to Calcutta. On arrival, he soon found many uses for his mercantile and managerial expertise. Eventually, his career embraced tax-collection, banking and politics, in addition to his vital role in pioneering colonial commerce. Despite local opposition, Campbell was able to identify colonial products which would be able to command export markets, possible staples of trade such as whale oil and sealskins. These were of the highly mobile, enterprising Scot. He gained employment as a medical officer in the East India Company, in whose service he learned the rudiments of commerce with which he made his first move to Australia in 1808. Building up his capital through trade, Berry pursued his ultimate objective, which was the acquisition of a large landed property in the colony. This he eventually attained at Shoalhaven in New South Wales, where he set himself up as laird to 386 tenants, upon whom he exercised an exquisitely nostalgic paternalism. Social aspirations blocked in Fife were now replicated in the colony, and Berry was fully satisfied with his success, achieved along the classic pathway from Scotland, by way of India and commerce, to wide acres in Australia.

The New Age of Free Settlement

The second and overlapping phase in the evolution of colonial Australia was the liberation of lands for free settlement, which accelerated in the 1820s. It was concomitant with the geographical extension of the colonies and the development of squatting, that is, the informal occupation of vast areas of the country by pastoralists. The success of the squatters, these great agrarian capitalists, depended on the retreat of the Aborigines, the extension of coastal and internal transport, the creation of export vents and, ultimately, the provision of an effective labour supply. Eventually, it became a development of continental scale, in which Scots played at least a proportional role.

Australia did not enter the age of mass international migration until the late 1830s. Indeed, until the passage of new land laws, the Ripon Regulations, in 1831, free settlement was extremely limited. Australia, for migrants, was too far away, it was tainted by convictism, and it had few economic prospects. Colonial land policy, until 1831, restricted the granting of territory to men with capital. Consequently, Scottish free settlers were mainly former officials, army officers on half pay, and merchants. Only very slowly did new blood from Scotland (or elsewhere) reach Australia. In the 1820s there were clear signs: in Van Diemen's Land, for instance, Scots constituted one sixth of the free settlers, and this proportion rose to a third in the following ten years. Among these convict- and emancipist-employing agriculturalists were men from both Highlands and Lowlands. But there was a preponderance of people squeezed by conditions in post-war Scottish farming — leaseholders and tenant farmers confronted by swollen rents and falling produce prices, short leases and insecurity of tenure by rationalizing landlords and the overburden of sub-tenants, or simply by too much competition and too many offspring. Some of them foresaw a loss of status in rural Scotland, others the chance of material advance in the colonies. Most would go to America or England, but some went to Australia.

From the Highlands the tacksmen felt most unsettled and had long found exit, often by prior military service, to permanent settlement abroad. The best Australian example, and an early one, was Major Donald Macleod of Talisker, scion of an illustrious family in Skye. In 1820, he at last sold off his lease, having served in the 56th Regiment, and sailed to Van Diemen's Land with his family of nine. On arrival, he was granted 2,000 acres on a property which he named 'Talisker', where he farmed until 1837 when he removed to Sydney. His third and fourth sons, not untypically, then became involved in another phase of pioneering. This was the 'Port Phillip Mania', led by Van Diemonians, with their livestock, taking over newly discovered territories inland from Port Phillip Bay. One of the Macleods squatted over 25,000 acres of pasture won from nature and the Aborigines after a series of sickening confrontations. In the long run, the Macleods emerged in the class of wealthy squatters who dominated so much of the newly settled regions of Australia by the 1840s, men who spread out southwards and westwards, waxing rich in producing wool for British industry.

Even in the earliest phase of free settlement in Australia, there was a wide variety of Scots — small merchants, professionals, labourers, servants, as well as farmers in search of new acres. Some of them emigrated under contract

Camels carrying wool.

(reminiscent of the older American system of indenturing). A Hobart employer in May 1823 was very pleased: 'Now there are so many Scotsmen arriving daily that I can get them for almost nothing'. With muscle and good fortune, there was money to be made in the outback for even the poorest immigrant. David Waugh wrote to his brother back in Edinburgh in 1834 that —

All the settlers are making money if they use common prudence. One Scotsman has been here 8 years, and came without a shilling, [and] cleared £1300 from his wool this last year, and so on with all the rest.

In these years, therefore, were established the first permanent links between Australia and Scotland, the first flows of free settlers and capital. As early as 1822, the Australian Company of Edinburgh and Leith was established. It was a prototype of corporate investment in Scottish/Australian commerce, and although relatively unsuccessful in itself, it was a forbear of much greater Scottish mercantile enterprise by mid century.

Gold Mania and Mass Migration

In the 1830s Australia at last emerged as a respectable destination for emigrants. It became a competitor in the great

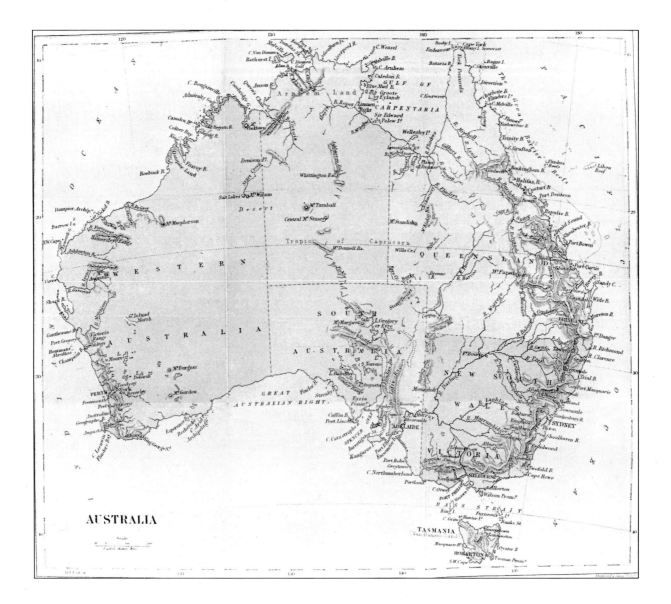

Map of Australia (1865).

28

international trade in humanity that rivalled commerce itself by the 1850s. The land system had been transformed, and the widening clutch of colonies was able to seek out and subsidize emigration in large numbers. Van Diemen's Land became a separate colony in 1825; South Australia in 1836; and Victoria in 1850. Convictism became increasingly unacceptable by the 1840s, and was terminated in most places by 1853. Western Australian colonization had begun early (in 1829), but struggled to sustain an independent population and continued to accept convicts until 1868. In 1890, its total population was still less than 50,000. Queensland began slowly and was not separated from New South Wales until 1859, when its population was still less than 30,000; it then accelerated and absorbed a growing proportion of Australian immigrants, especially those from Scotland.

Assistance to intending migrants varied in methods of selection, finance, nomination and land grants. But the systems of assistance gave Australia a special capacity to select its immigrants, and to exert an unusual degree of social engineering. High wages in Australia were a great attraction, much reinforced by the persuasion of emigration agents, several of whom traversed Scotland, including the Highlands and Islands. Many Scots emigrants had first to reach Liverpool or Plymouth before their departure, but others joined direct voyages from Greenock, Leith or Aberdeen. One of the most effective methods of recruitment of both assisted and private emigrants was by chain migration, usually prompted by letters from kinsfolk already in Australia. Many of these letters were published in Scottish newspapers.

The boom in colonization, especially in wool production, in the 1830s generated large demands for free labour, far beyond the capacity of the old convict economy. There was great inflation of wage rates especially in pastoral work. These demands coincided with news of famine and great distress in the West Highlands in 1836 and 1837. Scottish opinion in New South Wales caused Australian migration schemes to pay especial attention to the Highlands, which became a prime recruitment zone. Perhaps 10,000 Scots went to Australia between 1837 and 1842, many shipped directly from West Highland ports, organized by vigorous emigration agents who toured the north of Scotland and aroused great interest. The campaign brought the first great flows of Scots artisans and peasants to Australia (in company with many more from Ireland). The subsidization scheme demonstrated the possibility of reaching into the poorest echelons of society for emigrants who were prepared to cross the world to escape adverse conditions at home. Some of them arrived in a pitiful state and fell upon the mercy of private and public charity. But the link was now fully forged, and many of the early migrants succeeded well in the new land.

The greatest proponent of Scottish immigration in the 1830s was Dr J. D. Lang, who had been the first Presbyterian minister in New South Wales, arriving to join his brother in 1823, from the Evangelical wing of the Church of Scotland. He promoted his religion and values with fierce and noisy energy, and became a formidable political figure in mid-century New South Wales, regarded by some as the truest champion of freedom. He claimed repeatedly that the Scots were the most valuable of Australia's immigrants. At all time combative, he was the particular enemy of Catholicism. He set himself up against Irish female immigration which, he thundered in 1848, was 'silently subverting the Protestantism, and extending the Romanism of the colony through the vile, Jesuitical, diabolical system of mixed marriages'. Lang used his prodigious energies to raise the level of Scottish immigration and Presbyterianism in New South Wales. He promoted Calvinistic doctrines and challenged the Anglican domination of education in the colony. He raised the spectre of sectarianism in Australia, and was in the thick of every controversy, 'breathing fire, brimstone and eternal damnation against all who did not think exactly as he did'.

The bounty immigration system was swiftly terminated by the colonial economic crisis of 1841-42, one of many recurrent punctuations in the history of Australian immigration. Nevertheless, the use of revenues from land

CHAPTER III.

EFFECTS OF THE GOLD DISCOVERY.

THE excitement produced throughout the colonies, but especially in Sydney and Melbourne, by the publication of the gold discovery, may be inferred from the following facts : — In one week, upwards of 2,000 persons were counted on the road to the Bathurst diggings, and only eleven coming down. Hundreds of men, of all classes and conditions, threw up their situations, and leaving their wives and families behind them, started for the diggings. Whole crews ran away from their ships, which were left to rot in our harbours, the men having willingly forfeited all their wages, clothes, &c. Within one week, the prices of the following goods rose 25 per cent in Sydney :—flour, tea, sugar, rice, tobacco, warm clothing, and boots. Throughout all the towns, nothing was saleable but provisions, and diggers' tools and clothing. Every man who could handle a pick or spade was off, or preparing to be off, for the gold-fields. The roads were crowded with travellers, carriages, gigs, drays, carts, and wheelbarrows : mixed up in one confused assemblage might be seen magistrates, lawyers, physicians, clerks, tradesmen, and labourers.

Warehouses were shut, wages rose almost simultaneously throughout the country ; and in order to retain the services of persons in the public employment, Government found it neces-

sary to raise their pay. To the salaries of all junior clerks, an increase of 25 per cent. was made ; the pay of the police throughout the colony was also increased.

The building of houses, bridges, &c., was suspended for want of tradesmen, nearly all of them having gone to the diggings. Many houses might be seen half-finished for want of men to proceed with the work, though the owners or contractors were offering enormously high wages to any that would complete the works. The fields were left unsown—flocks of sheep were deserted by their shepherds. With one stockholder, who has 20,000 sheep, there remained only two men. Masters were seen driving their own drays ; and ladies of respectability and ample means were obliged to cook the family dinner. Servants and apprentices were off in a body ; and even the very " devils" bolted from the newspaper offices : in short, the yellow fever seized on all classes of society. In twenty-four hours, prices of provisions doubled at Bathurst and the neighbouring places. In all our steamers and trading vessels the rate of passage was raised, in consequence of the necessary increase in the wages of seamen. All the trades held their meetings, at which a new tariff of charges was agreed upon ; and even the publicans raised, at least 25 per cent., the prices of their wines, beer, and spirits.

Van Diemen's Land and New Zealand poured upon our shores shiploads of adventurers, attracted by the golden news ; and South Australia is now almost drained of its labouring population, one of the consequences of which is, that the shares in the famous Burra Burra copper-mines there have fallen from 230*l.* to 45*l.*,—a fall which has entailed ruin on hundreds.

In walking along the streets of Sydney or Melbourne, you hear nothing talked of but gold ; you see nothing exhibited in shop-windows but specimens of gold, or some article of equipment for the gold-digger. In every society, gold is the inter-

A description of the exodus to the goldfields, from David Mackenzie.
The Gold Digger. London, 1855.

Arrival of the Geelong Mail, Main Road, Ballarat, 1854, from W.B.
Withers. *History of Ballarat*. 2nd ed. Ballarat, 1887.

sales to subsidize immigration (in accord with the influential
ideas of Edward Gibbon Wakefield) remained the basic
policy for many decades, but increasingly co-ordinated by
more sophisticated methods of organization in selection
and shipping. Scotland was repeatedly criss-crossed by emigration agents from the Australian colonies, often in
competition not only against the United States and Canada
but also themselves.

The gold rushes caused a wild inrush of unorganized
immigration and frenetic outrushes of people from all parts
of Australia towards the Victorian and New South Wales
fields. Many Scots were involved and some of the gold camps
were identifiably Scottish; in Bendigo, it was said that every
gully had pipes and pipers. It was said that Scots were
prominent in the incipient radicalism in the gold-digging
fraternity often associated with the shortlived rebellion
against authority at the Eureka stockade. A Gaelic newspaper
also circulated briefly in 1857, and gave occasional expression to anti-landlord feeling among the émigré Highlanders.

Gold mania induced serious labour shortages in many
other parts of Australia, and various agencies in Britain,
private and public, responded to their needs. Once again

Stockman's hut, from *Rambles at the Antipodes*. London, 1859.

Australian labour demands created an opportunity to give relief to specially disadvantaged groups in Britain, notably the victims of the Irish famine. In 1852, the Colonial Land and Emigration Commissioners dispatched several Scottish groups equally seeking relief by means of emigration. They included many described as 'shepherds' (probably on the false assumption that all rural Highlanders were shepherds), and broadloom weavers from the Lowlands. In this way, emigration to Australia was again identified with declining elements in the Scottish economy. Similarly, the Scottish Australia Society was formed in Glasgow in July 1853, specifically to ameliorate the problems of redundant handloom weavers. The Victorian authorities sent an agent to Scotland to recruit 5,000 immigrants.

The greatest of the philanthropic schemes was that initiated by Charles Trevelyan, the Highland and Island Emigration Society, which was yet another effort to diminish the demographic and subsistence crisis in the north of Scotland, while simultaneously solving the labour problems of Australia. Trevelyan had fantasies of transmitting 40,000 Highlanders in unbroken families to Australia, sponsored by a combination of colonial, philanthropic and laird monies. However, during the brief life of the Society in the mid 1850s, only some 5,000 reached Australia. It was designed as a re-cycling system, whereby the emigrants would repay their passage after arrival, and the revenue would finance a further round of migration. The system did not succeed partly because of the difficulties faced by the migrants. Described on arrival in Australia as 'poverty stricken Gaels', the Highlanders made a distinctive addition to the colonial population. Some of them, notably a tragic contingent from the island of St Kilda, were decimated by disease and distress; some faced hostility, unemployment and disenchantment on their arrival. In June 1853, the Immigration Agent for Victoria, Edward Grimes, voiced some of the local criticism:

I do not consider that the inhabitants of the Islands of Scotland are well suited to the wants of the colony; their total ignorance of the English language renders it difficult to obtain employment for them, while their indolence and extremely filthy habits have occasioned a general impression against them.

Nevertheless, many eventually climbed the ladder to economic independence in Victoria, and some became extraordinarily successful in a material sense. In 1854, there were 1,500 Highlanders in Geelong alone, and several churches arose with their own Gaelic-speaking ministers. Generally, however, the immigrants tended to disperse and their language, and other distinctive aspects of their folk life, were not well sustained. It is clear that many of the Highlanders were motivated by a hunger for land: they took on wage labour or shepherding as the first step towards this goal. An intermediate stage was that of a tenancy under a large landowner before their savings had accumulated enough to secure their own independent farms. It was a process which required them to separate from their kinsfolk, and rendered any form of cultural solidarity extremely difficult to sustain. They had to adjust in other ways – there were few places in Australia where British, still less Highland, styles of farming could be reproduced. Farming was on a larger, more capital intensive scale, and all immigrant farmers were required to adapt to these conditions.

It is difficult to generalize about the expectations of such widely diversified Scots on reaching Australia. Personal

The Darling Downs.

testimony tended to emphasize the material prospects – for instance, those in the thoughts of Neil McCullum of Argyll, via Glasgow, who wrote from Geelong in 1854: 'I will be wealthier at the end of one year here than I was at the end of seventeen years of slavery' back in Scotland. Others had matrimonial ideas: indeed, to qualify for a free passage some Scots had negotiated very rapid marriages before their departure. Catherine Dickson, a domestic servant, after 14 years in Victoria, wrote home to her girlhood friends in Scotland: 'Tell them they will all get married if they come out here. Crippled ones, deaf and dumb females, all get married over here'.

Emigration diminished as the gold rushes subsided but revived strongly during several periods in the following fifty years. Special schemes, during times of renewed labour shortage, were directed to Scotland. Scots and, sometimes, Highlanders, were regarded with particular favour, but the Highland element probably diminished. From 1860 to 1919, about 58,000 Scots were assisted to Australia, some 13 per cent of the total (equivalent to their proportion in the British Isles). Now the lion's share, sometimes more than half, was taken by Queensland. Within the Scottish host, Lanarkshire, Edinburgh and Midlothian, followed by Aberdeenshire, Forfarshire and Ayrshire, dominated.

Scottish Squatters and Scottish Capital

Large-scale immigration created Scottish links across the continent, a tenuous network which sometimes favoured Scots as employees and investors. The connexions stretched back to Scotland, encouraging kinsfolk to form a chain of migration, promoting investment, arranging the appointment of ministers and teachers, and stimulating both rivalry and co-operation among these mobile Antipodean Scots. More permanent was the evident reciprocation of the Scottish and Australian economies. By 1860, Scottish savings were being channelled to Australasia in quite extraordinary quantities, often through the hands of great commercial companies and banks. Accordingly, the nexus between the two countries was welded more strongly.

The rural emphasis of the story continued. Many of the dynamic squatters of the mid century had amassed vast acreages and flocks and became pastoral kings. There were, among them, Scots who had seized opportunities for commercial profit in the highly capitalistic outback industry. Some of them established new dynasties in Australia, and became key men in the colonial political establishments. The success stories were legion, and help exemplify the relationship between Scotland and Australia. For instance, there was the case of George Russell, born in 1812, tenth of the thirteen children of a tenant farmer who had found economic conditions in Banchory, Aberdeenshire, and in Fife, gravely disappointing. There seemed little future on the land and the elder Russell, therefore, encouraged his sons to migrate. One brother left for Van Diemen's Land in 1821, and George Russell followed in 1831 to help manage the property there. In 1836, he crossed Bass Strait to the new settlements about Port Phillip. There he was employed by the Clyde Company, a group of Vandemonian Scottish pastoral capitalists. (They were also connected to Scottish mercantile capital in Glasgow, Edinburgh and Fife, and linked by family ties and useful political connexions.) In this matter, the outward-looking corporate enterprise employing the managerial experience of George Russell, was able to make effective claims on the new wilderness that would become Victoria. By 1839, Russell was managing 8,000 sheep for the Clyde Company, being paid £100 per annum and a share of the profits. It was a common method of payment and Russell (like so many of his upwardly mobile countrymen) was eventually able to set up on his own account and accumulate great riches. When he died in 1887 he left £318,000.

Some Scots succeeded with less corporate backing and without even the goad of relative poverty. John Peter was the first son of a prosperous family in Milngavie, with every prospect of respectable independence in his own country. Instead, he took off for New South Wales in 1832, his father paying his passage and giving him £50 to make a start. Helped by Scottish contacts on arrival, he soon found himself managing 2,000 sheep and a dozen assigned convicts on a large station on the Lachlan River. He felt isolated and oppressed by responsibility, yet succeeded well. An English contemporary remarked: 'You must recollect that he is a Scotchman which is in itself a sort of passport to fortune'. Peter was certainly canny. He married a rich widow and established himself as a pastoralist on the Murrumbidgee River, where he eventually generated an income of £40,000 a year: he bought a smart house in London and owned the lease of a shooting estate in the Highlands – each a badge of conspicuous consumption to rival the invading plutocracy of America in both places.

Such men as these were increasingly supported by direct capital investment from Scotland directed into primary producing industries in Australia. Even as early as the

1840s, the Royal Bank of Scotland was employing agents to seek out huge properties and newly discovered grazing lands in inland Australia. Scottish and Anglo-Scottish enterprises recruited Scottish managers or sent out men to represent them. The most successful of these — for example, Niel Black and the Hunter brothers — became themselves wealthy, ostentatious and powerful, entering political life and setting themselves up as colonial patriarchs.

Some minor Scottish aristocrats (and others with dubious or unorthodox claims to special social esteem) also emigrated to Australia. John Campbell of Tiree claimed familial connexions with the Duke of Argyll when he settled in South Australia, and John Macleod was described as the eleventh chief of Raasay, of the Clan Torquil, when he established a station at Narang with his brother. Some were clearly at the end of their ancestral line in Scotland, unable to maintain their status in their own land. The grandson of the Marquis of Ailsa emigrated as a manager in the service of a Scottish pastoral company, in which his father possessed an interest. In a way, Australia became a place to absorb these awkward surpluses produced by the Scottish economy. Most interesting of this class was Macdonell of Glengarry, a Highland chief in financial *extremis*. His West Highland estates were crippled with debt, and he sold out and headed for Australia in 1842, with a full entourage of followers and the residue of his capital. He believed that in Australia he would recover his fortune and presumably, his lost social status. He acquired a station in Gippsland and bought a great herd of dairy cattle. But the entire enterprise was quixotic because Glengarry and his Highlanders were totally unable to cope with the new conditions, or with the opposition of the local Aborigines. The enterprise collapsed. Glengarry returned home a forlorn and broken figure and died a few years later.

The Scots of Port Phillip were said to have made a ridiculous fuss over the arrival of Glengarry in 1842, and a great public dinner was arranged on St Andrew's Day. There was, indeed, a heightened sense of class and status among the Scots pastoralists. They devoted great energy to social

Angus McMillan.

elevation and the trappings of an émigré social status. And, though many Scots may have espoused a democratic spirit in their transfer to Australia, in reality it was rarely expressed in any obvious egalitarianism. Many of the successful Scots returned to Britain to demonstrate their fortune. And the case of Glengarry was not typical. Other Highlanders, more hard-headed men possessed of a more ruthless streak, did far better for themselves. Angus McMillan of Glenbrittle in Skye carved out a great personal fortune in the same district of Victoria though, in the process, he disposed of the Aborigines with hideous savagery.

While Australia grew well on its land and mineral resources, its future growth was directed increasingly to urban investment. The most notable evidence was the rise of 'Marvellous Melbourne', especially in the 1880s, but Sydney, Brisbane and Adelaide were not much less zestful. Scottish enterprise, inevitably, was heavily involved here, too. Australian Scots had emerged prominently in the colonial mercantile community. Some of the most illustrious names in late 19th-century mercantile capitalism were Scots. They included the great pastoral firms of Elders from Adelaide and Dalgety from Queensland, both servicing the rural sector with specialized managerial/provisioning expertise. Gilchrist and Alexander, Craig and Broadfoot, and Alexander Dick rose to early prominence in New South Wales. Alexander Brodie Spark was in the classic mould of blocked aspirations in Scotland. He left Elgin in 1811 and reached Sydney in 1823 via London and Van Diemen's Land. He entered local commerce and banking, and developed agency operations on behalf of various Scots enterprises in the Sydney market. He accumulated personal assets worth more than £40,000 by 1840, most of which, however, was swiftly liquidated in the colonial crash of 1841-42.

Australia attracted funds from Scotland and elsewhere by virtue of its high return on capital, and its relative stability as an expanding economy, with reasonably secure institutions and government. In the 1830s, there were reported returns on capital of 20 per cent and more per annum, though this was at the high risk end of the market. Generally, returns were normally much lower but held a sufficient margin to attract international funds. Aberdeen-based companies created a new initiative for Australian investment in the 1830s, reviving the notion of a Scottish network in mining and elsewhere. The North British Australasian Company, with a capital base of £50,000, began operations in Sydney in 1839, followed by the Scottish Australian Investment Company in 1840 with twice the capital. These were precursors of the international investment trusts which connected the small savers in Britain with high interest possibilities abroad, in America and, for the Scots, increasingly in Australia. Many of them were involved in the great mortgage business, which was vital for the exploitation on the international market of Australian primary resources. The critical function performed by these investment companies, which multiplied in the following decades, was to match the needs of savers in the United Kingdom with the credit requirements of producers in Australia. In this were demanded all the virtues of probity, reliability and confidence found in stable institutions and trusts, in the high calibre of the banking system, and improvements in commercial communications. In all these fields, Scots asserted a special influence in the Antipodes.

Thus, apart from the thousands of individual migrants who connected Scotland and Australia, there was an intricate web of capital and commerce between the two countries. It was a subtle relationship based upon the complementarity of their economies, and mediated by special mechanisms created on each side of the world. Essentially, the process began with the rising level of investible funds accumulating in Scotland by mid century. Small and large savings in Scotland, in both the countryside and in the towns, were mobilized by a remarkable cobweb of solicitors and chartered accountants, who gathered the funds for transmission through an agent to an Australian company. Edinburgh in the 1880s was said to have been honeycombed with these agencies working on behalf of overseas companies. In that decade, it was estimated that 40 per cent of Australian borrowings were raised through this channel. It was a system which tapped savings even in the remotest corners of Scotland, and was extraordinarily efficient in doing so. It saved Australia from total dependence on the London market, and helped to fuel the great boom in urban construction and capital works in Australia, prior to the great

Melbourne in 1875. *Australasian Sketcher,* 10 July 1875.

crash of 1893. By the late 1880s, more than a third of all Australian pastoral, mortgage and investment company securities were raised in Scotland.

All this meant that Scotland, despite recurrent financial collapses, reaped fruitful returns on her capital for many decades into the future. Scottish credit financed the commodity trade between the countries. For Australia, it consolidated its dependence on foreign capital, and on the volatility of the overseas investors' credit behaviour. For Scotland, these great investments represented the growing affluence of part of its economy, and may also have reflected the decline of investment opportunities at home. Australia, therefore, was not only an absorbent of Scotland's migrants but also of her surplus savings.

The Australian banking system was often influenced by Scottish practice, and many colonial bankers were Scots, who continued to recruit further employees from Scotland. Similarly, many Scots were involved directly in colonial property finance, and especially in the frenetic speculative activity which eventually undermined the great financial boom of the late 1880s. Some were known for their public probity and Presbyterian rectitude – there is, indeed, a well known argument that Calvinism put a certain steel into the Scots by equating individual virtue with material success. But there were also cases of commercial rapacity and double standards in personal morality, which may suggest that Scottish Australian morality was close to general colonial norms. For Scotland, emigration to Australia was clearly a vehicle for the advance of Scots abroad and for the export of capital. But whether it produced any direct benefit to Scots industry has been doubted, since it created few permanent markets for Scottish products.

The Scottish Presence in Australia

It would be absurd to reduce the relationship between Scotland and Australia to exclusively economic matters. Some of the most important connexions were entirely intellectual, cultural or theological. There were intangible and formative Scottish elements in the complicated evolution of Australian education. Some of the influences were transmitted in general mentalities which were beyond measurement. Presbyterian varieties of worship and dispute were exported to the new continent, frequently in the severest forms. Schisms in the Church in Scotland, especially in its Evangelical wing, were visited on the Scots emigrants, notably during the Disruption. Sometimes the sea-divided Scots regarded the events in Scotland with scarcely disguised incomprehension.

Missionary Scots cast an influence on Aboriginal culture, and the Kirk was the most vigorous instrument of all in perpetuating and stimulating Scottish culture abroad. Against this was the demonstrable slide of many successful Australian Scots into Anglicanism as their affluence took them into the higher reaches of colonial social status. Similarly, extreme Sabbath observance and a vein of ostentatious righteousness created tensions and accusations of hypocrisy.

Some Scots were conscious cultural missionaries, who brought with them the superior achievements of Scottish education. Many observers believed that the Scots were the most single-minded and successful of Australia's immigrants. Anthony Trollope said in 1873: 'They now form an established aristocracy, with very conservative feelings, and are quickly becoming as firm a country party as that which is formed by our squirearchy at home'. Some of the great Scots pastoral families wielded continuing social and political influence, especially in parts of western Victoria and also elsewhere, even into the 20th century.

Yet it is difficult to demonstrate conclusively any differential success of the Scots in Australia. There were sectors, however, where there was a visible disproportion. For instance, though Scots were not more than 16 per cent of the overseas-born in Victoria in the late 19th century, they constituted about 30 per cent of all members of the Victorian parliament. It is likely that, of the pastoral pioneers in each of the colonies, the Scots were also over-represented; but in other areas of Australian life, the disproportion was probably less.

Finally, though Scots tended not to create local concentrations of their own kind, they were, nevertheless, sufficiently self-conscious to perpetuate their old identity. Local Scottish patriotisms were cultivated and expressed in various ways. St Andrew's societies were formed in Victoria as early as 1846, and there was a veritable spate of new foundations at the time of the gold rushes. Often these bodies adopted a pronounced Highland colouring, no doubt to emphasize their distinctiveness and to gain collective solace from the separation from Scotland. Again, at the turn of the century, there was a further efflorescence: seventeen new societies were formed in Victoria alone between 1906 and 1910, associated with other outward forms such as a proliferation of Burns statues, societies to regulate and promote Scottish sports, and newspapers and magazines to promote Scottish Australia.

In general, the collective efforts of these Australian Scots were designed to sustain a measure of Scottish fraternity and identity against the grain of its gradual dissolution. It was a conscious effort to resist the homogenization of Scots into a society which was being dominated by what were considered as specifically English forms. In the longer run, even this mildly political attitude was overtaken as both Scots and English blended into a separately identifiable Australian psyche and culture.

Captain James Cook, whose father was a Lowland Scot.

A SETTLEMENT IN BOTANY BAY

A PLAN has been formed, by my direction, for transporting a number of convicts, in order to remove the inconvenience which arose from the crowded state of the gaols in different parts of the kingdom; and you will, I doubt not, take such farther measures as may be necessary for this purpose.

With these words, King George III announced in his Speech to Parliament, on 23 January 1787, the Government's intention to start transporting criminals to the distant territory of New South Wales, which had been possessed for Britain by Captain James Cook only sixteen years previously.

On 13 May 1787, the eleven ships of the First Fleet—nine transports and storeships under the escort of HMS *Sirius* and HMS *Supply*—set out from Portsmouth on their 15,000-mile voyage to New South Wales, half a globe away. On board the transports were approximately 600 male and 200 female convicts, with four companies of marines to guard them. Captain Watkin Tench, a marine officer on board the convict transport *Charlotte*, described the Fleet's departure in his *Narrative of the Expedition to Botany Bay*, published in 1789:

I strolled down among the convicts, to observe their sentiments at this juncture. A very few excepted, their countenances indicated a high degree of satisfaction, though in some the pang of being severed, perhaps for ever, from their native land, could not be wholly suppressed; in general marks of distress were more perceptible among the men than the women.

In charge of the expedition was Captain Arthur Phillip, the English naval officer who had been appointed Governor of the new settlement. His second-in-command was a Scot from Leith, John Hunter, Second Captain of the *Sirius*, who

was to succeed him as Governor in 1795. Under the supervision of these humane and experienced officers, only about one in thirty of the convicts died throughout the long ordeal of the voyage, and, of these, many had been in poor health when they boarded the transports. Hunter recorded in his journal, published in London in 1793 under the title *An Historical Journal of the Transactions at Port Jackson*, the Governor's command that the irons be taken off the male convicts: 'that they might have it more in their power to strip their cloaths off at night when they went to rest, be also more at ease during the day, and have the farther advantage of being able to wash and keep themselves clean'.

After calling at Rio de Janeiro and the Cape of Good Hope for stores, the Fleet sailed on, surviving many difficulties and dangers during the eight-month voyage. By mid-January 1788, the ship carrying the Governor had arrived at Botany Bay, to be followed soon after by the other vessels. 'The wind was now fair, the sky serene...and the temperature of the air delightfully pleasant: joy sparkled in every countenance. To us it was a great, an important day...', wrote Watkin Tench in his *Narrative*. Finding Botany Bay unsuitable as a place of settlement, Phillip continued north to Port Jackson and chose another bay, which he named Sydney Cove. There, on 26 January 1788, now celebrated as Australia Day, a party from the ships landed.

Just over one thousand people – the Governor and his staff, officials, convicts, marines and a few of their wives and families – now had to create a settlement in a wilderness. Conditions were harsh for all, but the sufferings endured by the convicts, some of whom had to do the work of draught

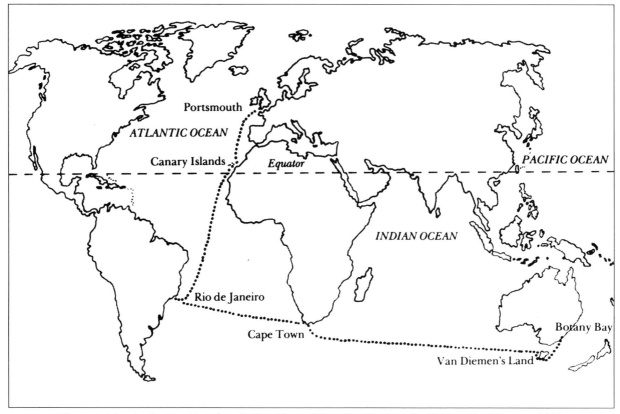

The route taken by the First Fleet, from Barbara Vance Wilson. *Convict Australia, 1788-1868*. Melbourne, 1981.
By permission of Oxford University Press, Melbourne.

animals, were underlined in the 'Surgeon's Return of the Sick' of June 1788, published in *The Voyage of Governor Phillip to Botany Bay* in 1789. Only five months after the landing, twenty-eight male and female convicts were dead, also eight 'convict children', and sixty-six were receiving medical treatment. The remainder, under threat of the lash, had been put to work clearing the land and cutting timber for building. Capable and determined, Governor Phillip and Captain Hunter had drawn up plans, and the township at Sydney Cove was beginning to take shape. As the Governor wrote in his account published in *The Voyage:*

There are few things more pleasing than the contemplation of order and useful arrangement arising gradually out of tumult and confusion; and perhaps this satisfaction cannot anywhere be more fully enjoyed than where a settlement of civilized people is fixing itself upon a newly discovered or savage coast.

In one of the earliest maps of Sydney Cove, drawn in part by

Governor John Hunter.

Scottish origin over the sixty-year history of transportation. Scots were not more upright than their English or Irish counterparts, but the attitude of Scottish judges to transportation differed from that of English judges. In Scotland, it was believed that transportation was a savage punishment, carrying with it a grave risk of death from the hardships of the passage to New South Wales, so such sentences were only given reluctantly. Transportation was also disliked by those in Scotland who had painful memories of its use in the aftermath of the Jacobite Risings. Of the total of 5,500 men and 2,200 women transported from Scotland, Donnachie's researches show that their average age was twenty-five, the majority were single and poor, and around three-quarters were punished for crimes against property.

Thomas Watling was a convict of a different order. He was born in 1762 in Dumfries and was trained as an artist, before being arrested on a charge of having forged guinea notes of the Bank of Scotland, at that time a capital offence. Maintaining his innocence, Watling petitioned to be transported rather than stand trial, and received a sentence of fourteen years. After fifteen bitter months of imprisonment awaiting transportation, Watling reached New South Wales in 1792, and was immediately assigned to the service of the Surgeon-General, John White.

Watling was the first professional artist to live and work in the colony, and he spent the next few years drawing and painting natural history subjects for his master. His water-colours form a unique historical record of life in the new land, and are distinguished by their vividness and technical skill. In them, he portrayed what he saw around him — the tattooed Aborigines, their artefacts and boats, the wild animals, birds and flowers, strange in shape and colour. His works form part of the 'Watling Collection' in the British Museum (Natural History) — a one-volume collection of over five hundred drawings made by several artists, apparently before 1794, in and around Port Jackson. One hundred and twenty-three of the drawings are signed by Thomas Watling,

Captain Hunter in July 1788, ground is carefully marked out for the Governor's House, and for the Church, the Hospital, the Observatory and the Criminal Court.

The proportion of Scots in the convict population of the colony was never large. As Ian Donnachie clearly demonstrates,[1] only around one in twenty convicts was of

1. Ian Donnachie. 'Scottish Criminals and Transportation to Australia, 1786-1852', *Scottish Economic and Social History,* iv (1984), pp.21-38.

'An east view of Port-Jackson and Sydney Cove', by Thomas Watling. *By permission of the British Museum (Natural History).*

and others appear to be in his style. Watling's gifts were not solely artistic, for he wrote and had published in England, in 1794, *Letters from an Exile at Botany Bay to his Aunt in Dumfries*. In these letters, he gives lively descriptions of the climate, countryside and native customs of New South Wales:

The air, the sky, the land, are objects entirely different from all that a *Briton* has been accustomed to see before . . . The men and women, at an early age, devote to their chieftain, the former, one of the upper fore-teeth; and the latter, the first joint of the little finger of the left hand, as a token of their fidelity . . . The hair smeared with gum, and forked as the porcupine; a bone or straw stuck horizontally through the middle cartilege [sic] of the nose; and the body streaked over with red or white earth completes the *ton* of dress of the inhabitants of N.S. Wales, either for war, love or festivity.

Bitterly resentful of his position as 'the property of a haughty despot', Watling was at last pardoned when the Scot, John Hunter, was appointed Governor in 1795, and he was free to leave the colony. During his servitude Watling had had a son, presumably by a convict woman, and he took the boy with him to India, where he worked for three years as a miniature painter in Calcutta. Then he returned to Dumfries, only to be charged again in 1806 with forging Bank of Scotland notes, but a 'Not proven' verdict was returned. A few

Aborigines going to a meeting with the Governor, 1790, from the 'Watling Collection'. *By permission of the British Museum (Natural History).*

Linen scarf or neckerchief, apparently produced in Scotland after the trial of Thomas Muir and his associates. *By permission of the Mitchell Library, State Library of New South Wales.*

years later he sent a dignified appeal for financial assistance to his old Governor, John Hunter, by then an Admiral living in retirement in London, in which he revealed that he had 'a disorder of the cancerous kind'. His letter was found among Hunter's papers, but the result of his appeal is not known. Thereafter, Watling passes out of recorded history, and the date and place of his death are unknown.

Another notable convict in the early settlement was Thomas Muir of Huntershill, one of a group of five political reformers known as the 'Scottish Martyrs' (although, in fact, only two were Scots). The only son of a wealthy Glasgow merchant, he was born in 1765 and was educated at the University of Glasgow, thereafter becoming a lawyer and a member of the Faculty of Advocates. A man of high ideals and a devout Christian, Muir and his fellow Scot, William Skirving, were prominent in the agitation for political reform in the years after the outbreak of the French Revolution. The group was charged with sedition by a frightened government, put on trial in Edinburgh, and, despite public protest, sentenced to fourteen years' transportation.

Muir, Skirving and two of the other 'Martyrs' arrived in New South Wales in 1794. They were treated as special prisoners by the Lieutenant-Governor, who was acting on the British Government's instructions, and were free of restraint within the colony, provided they did not take part in political activity. Muir and Skirving, being men of substance, were able to purchase farms, and, thereafter, Muir devoted himself to intellectual pursuits. Only one of Muir's letters survives from his time in the convict settlement. It was written on 13 December 1794 to his friend Mr Moffat, a solicitor in London, and is printed in Peter Mackenzie's *Life of Thomas Muir*, published in Glasgow in 1831:

I am pleased with my situation, as much as a man can be, separated from all he loved and respected ... of our treatment here, I cannot speak too highly. Gratitude will forever bind me to the officers, civil and military.

Skirving, worn out with labour on his farm and grieving at the separation from his family, died in 1796.

Monument to Thomas Muir and the 'Scottish Martyrs' in the Old
Calton Burying Ground, Edinburgh.

Alone of the 'Martyrs', Muir managed to escape from the colony on an American vessel, but ill-fortune pursued him throughout an adventurous journey to freedom via Nootka Sound, Mexico, Cuba and Spain. On the final part of his voyage, near Cadiz, the Spanish frigate to which he had transferred was attacked by two English vessels, and Muir had one eye and part of his face shot off. He finally reached the haven of revolutionary France, but his health was broken and he died there in 1799, aged only thirty-three.

The courage and sacrifice of Thomas Muir and his companions, whose democratic ideas of parliamentary reform and universal suffrage were far in advance of their time, are commemorated by a monument in the Old Calton Burying Ground in Edinburgh, which bears Muir's own words:

I have devoted myself to the cause of the People; it is a good cause; it shall ultimately prevail; it shall finally triumph.

In 1820, a second group of political prisoners, known as the Scottish Radicals, was transported to the colony for taking part in a small-scale uprising against the government, in the course of which the rebels had tried to set up a Provincial Government for Scotland. The insurrection, which was provoked by poverty, hunger and unemployment, was led by weavers, whose rallying cry was 'Scotland Free – or a Desert', but it was speedily crushed by the authorities. Two of the leaders, Andrew Hardie of Glasgow and John Baird of Condorrat, were executed at Stirling, and nineteen other men convicted of high treason had their sentences commuted to transportation.

Unlike most of their fellow-convicts, the Scottish Radicals were respectable, skilled and literate, and they made a positive contribution to the life of the colony. Most of them prospered – John Anderson, a native of Camelon near Falkirk, taught for thirty-four years at the Presbyterian school at Portland Head; Allan Murchie from Dunfermline became the licensee of a public house named 'The Help Me Thro' the World' in Sydney; and Andrew Dawson from Stirlingshire became Principal Overseer of Works at Newcastle. Alexander Hart from Old Kilpatrick settled to his trade of cabinet-making, and many years later, he and his wife wrote home from Sydney: 'We both like the country well and shall be satisfied to end our Journey here if such is the will of Providence'.

From the beginning Scots played a significant part in the administration of the settlement. Three of the first six governors of New South Wales were Scots – John Hunter (1795-1800), Lachlan Macquarie (1810-1821) and Sir Thomas Makdougall Brisbane (1821-1825) – but less exalted figures were also prominent. Many Scottish soldiers occupied positions of authority, including William Paterson from Montrose, who commanded the New South Wales Corps in 1794 and was later to be Lieutenant-Governor, a post which became almost a Scottish preserve. The Commissariat was largely staffed by Scots, such as Andrew Miller, the first Commissary, and William Lithgow, educated at the University of Edinburgh, who arrived in 1824 to set up the accounts branch, and later became Auditor-General. It was, however, in the ranks of the civil administration that Scots were most numerous, working in the fields of medicine, law, engineering, public works and surveying, and often using their influence to assist their fellow-countrymen. After 1820, a trickle of free settlers – men who could raise the passage money of forty guineas steerage or seventy guineas for cabin passage, and had a minimum capital of five hundred pounds – began to arrive in New South Wales. The Scots amongst these settlers included officers pensioned off after the Napoleonic Wars, younger sons of the landed gentry anxious to improve their prospects, and merchants seeking wider spheres for their enterprise. Two merchants who were already there and who were to have an important influence on the colony's future economic development were Robert Campbell from Ayrshire and Alexander Berry from Fife, about whom accounts are given in Chapter 5.

New South Wales made significant progress after Major-General Lachlan Macquarie became Governor in 1810. He was born on Ulva near Mull in the Inner Hebrides in 1762, a younger son of the cousin of the chieftain of Clan Macquarie. Joining the Army at the age of fifteen, he campaigned in the West Indies, North America and India, rising through the ranks to become commanding officer of the 73rd Highlanders. In 1808, a rebellion against Governor William Bligh had occurred in New South Wales, and the British government had appointed Brigadier-General Miles Nightingall as Governor in his place, ordering the 73rd Regiment under Macquarie to accompany him to Sydney. When ill-health forced Nightingall to resign before his departure, Macquarie applied for and was given the post of Governor. His wife, Elizabeth Henrietta Campbell, a relation of the Earl of Breadalbane, accompanied him to Sydney. Intending to remain for a brief period only, Macquarie served until 1821, one of the longest and most successful Governors in the colony's history.

He found New South Wales demoralized and faction-ridden, with public buildings decaying and public morals in decline. Strongly conscious of the responsibilities of his

Lachlan Macquarie, Governor of New South Wales, 1810-1821.
By permission of the Mitchell Library, State Library of New South Wales.

office, Macquarie set about transforming the convict settlement. The administration was regularized, a programme of public works was instituted, and schools, hospitals, churches and roads were constructed. Exploration was encouraged and new land opened for colonization.

A central feature of Macquarie's administration was his humanitarian policy towards ex-convicts. 'When once a prisoner should have become free (through the expiation of his offence) his former state should no longer be remembered', he wrote in April 1817 to Henry Bathurst, the Colonial Secretary. Emancipists of merit were appointed to the public service and were even, on occasion, entertained at Government House. The Governor's efforts to transform the miserable penal settlement into a self-respecting colony by encouraging emancipist participation in affairs aroused the indignation of some officials, free settlers and military officers, who refused to associate with ex-convicts. Protests that Macquarie's administration was extravagant, and that he was weakening the effect of transportation as a punishment, poured into the Colonial Office. His detractors in London even presented a petition to Parliament in 1817, scurrilously accusing him of seizing land, interfering with justice and making life easy for convicts. In 1819, the Government sent Commissioner J. T. Bigge to New South Wales to inquire into the conduct of affairs, but conflict soon arose between him and Macquarie, who was angered by criticisms made by a man who had no direct experience of the colony. Finding, like many governors before and after him, that he had sacrificed his health and his peace of mind in the fulfilment of his office, Macquarie finally resigned in 1821.

A complex man, dutiful and narrow, but kindly and sensitive, Macquarie was supported and encouraged by his cultivated wife Elizabeth, who herself had worked to improve the lot of female convicts, orphans and Aborigines. With her, he made several journeys in New South Wales and Van Diemen's Land, and his prediction, 'My name will not readily be forgotten', was fulfilled, for many towns and streets bear his or Elizabeth's name in the country which he was the first governor to call 'Australia' in his official dispatches.

Mrs Macquarie's Seat.

On his return to Britain, Macquarie was granted a pension but was denied recognition and a title. Bigge's far from objective reports, criticising his building programme and his encouragement of emancipists, were published after the Governor left the colony, and were deeply resented by Macquarie, who was not allowed to reply publicly. Disillusioned by the lack of recognition of his forty-seven years of public service, and in failing health through fever caught in India, Macquarie died in London in 1824. No obituary appeared in *The Times*, although the news of his death caused profound public sorrow when it reached the colony. He was buried on the island of Mull, where the epitaph on his tombstone reads:

Here, in the hope of a glorious resurrection, Lie the Remains of the late MAJOR GENERAL LACHLAN MACQUARIE, of Jarvisfield, who was born 31st January 1761, and died at London, on the 1st of July 1824.

He was appointed Governor of New South Wales, AD 1809, and for 12 years fulfilled the duties of that situation, with eminent ability and

Elizabeth Macquarie. *By permission of the Tasmanian Museum and Art Gallery.*

success. His services in that capacity have justly attached a lasting honour to his name ... the rapid improvement of the Colony under his auspices and the high estimation in which both his Character and Government were held, rendered him truly deserving of the appellation ... *The Father of Australia.*

Macquarie's successor as Governor in 1821 was also a professional soldier, Sir Thomas Makdougall Brisbane, who came from a landed family in Largs in Ayrshire. A commanding figure, this 'mild and pleasant man' inherited a colony still bedevilled by the divisions between free and freed. Following government policy, Brisbane encouraged settlement by easier land grants and reorganized the administration of the convict system. During his term of office, the absolute nature of the Governor's authority was modified by the establishment of a Legislative Council and independent law courts, trial by jury in civil proceedings was introduced, and press censorship lifted.

An active Christian, Brisbane did much to advance the work of churches of all denominations in the colony. 'There is no object I have more sincerely at heart, than the advancement of morality in these colonies, where unhappily ... there is a wide and most extensive field to act upon', he wrote in a private letter of June 1824. No action by the Governor, however, was without its critics. He had to contend with disloyal officials, greedy settlers and arrogant magistrates. One of his sternest critics was the young Dr John Dunmore Lang from Greenock, who had arrived in Sydney in 1823 as the city's first Presbyterian minister, and who soon clashed with the Governor over the treatment of his church. Malicious articles in the British press added to Brisbane's difficulties. 'Sir Thomas spends the greater part of his time in his Observatory, or shooting parrots', wrote one newspaper.

Brisbane's passion was astronomy. In 1822, at his own expense, he built an Observatory behind Government House in Parramatta, calling it 'the Greenwich of the southern hemisphere'. Observations taken there were later published in 1835 as *A Catalogue of 7385 Stars Chiefly in the Southern Hemisphere.* For his services to astronomy, the Governor had

Sir Thomas Makdougall Brisbane.

received the Gold Medal of the Astronomical Society. At the presentation ceremony in London, in 1828, the President of the Society, Sir John Herschel, was to describe Brisbane as 'the founder of Australian science'. He also established the Philosophical Society of New South Wales, and was its first President.

Two of Brisbane's four children were born during his time in New South Wales, and they were named Thomas Australius and Eleanor Australia in honour of their place of birth. Sadly, all four children were to predecease him. His Christian faith supported him throughout his life, as was shown when his *Reminiscences* were posthumously published in Edinburgh in 1860. In September 1823 he had written:

Have had many difficulties with which to contend, arising principally from the male population... I can avow before the Author of my being... that I have never done an act whilst here, which I considered displeasing to God or unjust to my fellow-man...[I] desire only to be an engine in the Divine hand for the temporal good and the eternal welfare of all in the colony.

When Brisbane was recalled in 1825, he left a colony in which significant political progress had been made, despite the defects in his administration. In a letter dated 25 June 1825, he was able to tell Sir Walter Scott that 'the colony is certainly flourishing', and as his *Reminiscences* indicate, he remained convinced throughout his long life that a great future lay before Australia.

'IT WAS A VAST BLANK'[1]

BEHIND the first settlement made in 1788 at Sydney Cove, on the south-east coast of New South Wales, lay a virtually unknown continent as vast as the United States of America. The exploration of the 2,975,000 square mile interior of Australia was slowly accomplished during the 19th century, and it involved a number of great journeys of discovery in which Scottish travellers and scientists played an important part. The books they wrote about their journeys were notable contributions to the literature of Australian exploration.

The first inland explorers of New South Wales were Governor Arthur Phillip and Captain John Hunter who, despite their official duties, found time to satisfy their curiosity about the land that lay around them. Travelling on foot, the two men and their escort 'with great labour' made their way through the thick forests and hills around the colony, and frequently met the native tribes on their journeys. On one occasion, Phillip nearly lost his life when he approached a group of Aborigines with arms outstretched. Mistaking his intentions, one threw a spear which lodged in the Governor's shoulder – an encounter which is vividly depicted in a watercolour in the 'Watling Collection'. Of the Aborigines, Hunter wrote in his *Historical Journal*:

We wished to live with them on the most friendly footing, and ... to promote, as much as might be in our power, their comfort and happiness.

In June 1789 Governor Phillip, with Hunter, discovered an important river in New South Wales, naming it the Hawkesbury after the Earl of Liverpool, Baron Hawkesbury. Later that month, the two men set out on a journey to explore the river more extensively, in the course of which Phillip discovered and named Richmond Hill. On 5 July 1789, Hunter wrote:

In the morning, we walked to the top of the hill, and found we were not more than five or six miles from a long range of mountains ... this range of mountains we supposed to be those which are seen from Port Jackson, and called the Blue Mountains ... [the hill] on which we stood was called Richmond-hill.

As well as exploration by land, voyages were made to explore the bays around the coast. 'In the end of August, the Governor having expressed a wish to have a survey made of Broken-Bay and Botany-Bay, I offered to perform that service', Hunter noted in 1789.

An important contribution to the seaborne exploration of Australia was made by Forres-born Lieutenant James Grant, commander of the *Lady Nelson*. This ship left England in March 1800, and was the first vessel to sail along the entire southern coastline of Australia, and to pass eastward through the Bass Strait between the mainland and Van Diemen's Land. Grant arrived in the colony in December 1800. In March 1801, he was ordered to the Hunter River, seventy miles north of Sydney, and became one of the first Europeans to explore that river. He recorded many new facts about the natural history of the area and the customs of the

---

1. *South Australian Advertiser*, 22 January 1863.

native inhabitants, which he incorporated in his *Narrative of a Voyage of Discovery Performed in His Majesty's Vessel The Lady Nelson*, published in London in 1803.

Later in 1801, Grant resigned and the command of the *Lady Nelson* passed to Lieutenant John Murray, who claimed to have been born in Edinburgh. After surveying the Bass Strait, Murray sailed westward along the south coast of Australia and, on 14 February 1802, discovered and took formal possession of what is now Port Phillip Bay in Victoria. While the *Lady Nelson* was anchored inside the Bay, Murray made several exploratory journeys on shore, and was responsible for naming a local landmark Arthur's Seat.

Several Scots took part in the botanical exploration of the new continent, one of the first being Robert Brown (1773-1858), the son of an Episcopalian minister. He was born in Montrose and was educated at the University of Edinburgh, where he studied medicine but did not graduate. In 1795, Brown obtained a commission in the Fifeshire Regiment of Fencibles as an assistant surgeon, but he found army life uncongenial. His primary interest was natural history, and he entered into a correspondence on this subject with Sir Joseph Banks, the wealthy patron of botanical research who had accompanied Captain Cook to the South Seas in the *Endeavour*. In 1800, to Brown's delight, Banks offered him the post of naturalist on board the *Investigator*, which was being prepared for a scientific expedition to survey the coasts of Australia. 'The situation of naturalist to the New Holland expedition I will most cheerfully accept of' Brown replied to Banks, in a letter dated 17 December 1800.

The *Investigator*, under the command of Captain Matthew Flinders, arrived in Australian waters in December 1801, and for the next three and a half years the twenty-eight-year-old Brown devoted himself to botanical collecting around the coasts and islands of the continent. Acutely observant and dedicated to his work, he gathered approximately 3,400 specimens (more than half of which were new to science), and built up an unrivalled knowledge of the flora of the country. Brown left Australia for ever in May 1805, 'in the crazy low cut down *Investigator*, perhaps the most

Robert Brown. *By permission of the British Museum (Natural History).*

Allan Cunningham.

volume was published: it was a commercial failure, selling, it is said, only 26 copies of the 250 printed, although a supplement containing additional material appeared in 1830. Brown also wrote a botanical appendix to Matthew Flinders' *Voyage to Terra Australis*, published in 1814.

In 1810, Brown became librarian to Sir Joseph Banks. Ten years later, he inherited Banks's library and herbarium, which he agreed to transfer to a new department in the British Museum in 1827, under his own direction. He received many honours for his work — in 1811 he had been made a Fellow of the Royal Society, and he was President of the Linnean Society from 1849 to 1853 — and he was also offered chairs at the Universities of Edinburgh and of Glasgow, which he declined. His interest in Australian botany continued throughout his long life, and his last work was an appendix to the English explorer Charles Sturt's *Narrative of an Expedition into Central Australia*, published in London in 1849. Brown remained Keeper of the Botanical Collections in the British Museum until his death in 1858. He was an outstanding figure in the scientific world of his time, and his friend and physician, Dr Francis Boott, later wrote of him in a letter subsequently published in D. J. Mabberley's biography, *Jupiter Botanicus: Robert Brown of the British Museum* (1985):

I never presumed to be able to estimate Brown's eminent merits as a man of science, but I knew vaguely their worth; I loved him for his truth, his singular modesty … Of all the persons I have known, I have never known his equal in kindliness of nature.

It was through the agency of Robert Brown and Sir Joseph Banks that, in 1814, a young clerk at Kew named Allan Cunningham (1791-1839), the son of a Renfrewshire gardener, was appointed a botanical collector to the Royal Gardens. Cunningham spent the next two years of his life gathering specimens in Brazil, and then was ordered to New South Wales where he arrived, armed with a manuscript copy of Brown's great *Prodromus*, at the end of 1816. 'Mr Allan Cunningham, King's Botanist' made a good impression on

deplorable ship in all the world', as he wrote in an unpublished paper. It was a 'tedious and uncomfortable passage', with the damp conditions of the unseaworthy vessel always threatening his collection, but he reached Liverpool safely in October 1805.

Brown spent the next four years writing up his work, and in 1810 the *Prodromus Florae Novae Hollandiae*[1] was published. It was, in the words of his contemporary, Sir William Hooker, 'the greatest botanical work that has ever appeared'. The book was written in Latin but only the first

---

1. [*Preliminary Work on the Flora of New Holland.*]

Governor Macquarie, who the following year encouraged him to join Surveyor-General John Oxley's expedition into the country west of the Blue Mountains to explore the Lachlan River. Oxley believed that by following the river to its source, he would arrive at a great inland sea, but the river, in fact, disappeared into marshes. The disappointed explorer concluded that the interior of 'this singular continent' was one interminable swamp.

For Cunningham, the 1,200-mile expedition, which took from April to September to complete, introduced him to a new world of natural history. The journey took him first through undulating country, over ridges clothed with twisted eucalyptus, through valleys with great kangaroo herds, and on into an area that was barren and covered with brushwood. On 25 April 1817, he recorded in his 'Journal'[1] his meeting with the Lachlan River Aborigines, in whom he was greatly interested:

By way of ornament they wore Kangaroo teeth in their ears and cockatoo feathers in their hair. Those of them who were young men had their beards divided into three divisions and formed into plaited tails...I presented one with an English halfpenny having a hole drilled through it. It was, however, returned to me with clear signs that a piece of kangaroo flesh would be more acceptable.

Many of the entries in the 'Journal' are concerned with his botanical activities:

Took a walk a short distance on [sic] the Camp, gathered seeds of *Patersonia sericea; Goodenia sp.*, a small herbaceous plant, and a species of *Hypoxis*, a small liliaceous plant, found among grass.

On another occasion, Cunningham notes, 'We shot some of the new cockatoos today, but found their flesh hard and rancid'. The hazardous journey, in which the explorers 'suffered much from thirst', provided Cunningham with specimens of over 400 plant species, but more significantly, it awakened in him the desire to become an explorer as well as a botanical student of the unknown mountains, plains and rivers of the new country.

During the next five years, Cunningham made a succession of voyages which took him to the north and north-west coasts of Australia, and also to the islands of the Great Barrier Reef and Tasmania, where he landed frequently to collect plant specimens. Between expeditions, he concentrated on the botany of New South Wales until in March 1823, encouraged by Governor Brisbane, he began the series of journeys of exploration for which his name is best remembered. In 1823, he discovered Pandora's Pass, the great route of communication between Bathurst, the Hunter River and the Liverpool Plains, and the account of his journeys was published in London in 1825 in *Geographical Memoirs on New South Wales by Various Hands*, edited by Barron Field. His exploration of the Liverpool Plains in 1825 was followed two years later by the most important of all his expeditions, which took place between January and August 1827. Cunningham and his party of six men and eleven packhorses left the Hunter Valley and travelled north. They hacked a path for the horses through dense thickets, and crossed the Peel and Dumaresq Rivers, spurred on by the sight of a 'luxuriant growth of grass'. On 5 June, Cunningham reached a vantage point from which he saw an unforgettable sight, described in the report he made of his journey on 6 June 1827 –

...downs of a rich, black and dry soil, clothed with abundance of grass ... constituting a range of sound sheep pasture convenient to water but beyond the reach of floods ... Such is the character of Darling Downs which comprise little short of 28,000 acres.

By discovering this rich pastureland, he gave impetus to the northward expansion of the colony into an entirely new area of settlement, part of the future colony of Queensland.

Cunningham, whose health was deteriorating, requested permission to return to Britain and left the colony in 1831, but the following year he was offered the post of Colonial Botanist when the holder, Charles Frazer from Blair Atholl, died. Cunningham declined the position in favour of his younger brother Richard, who worked at Kew and was

---

1. Now in the British Museum (Natural History), London.

Cunningham's Gap.

familiar with the botany of Australia. Richard Cunningham reached Sydney in 1833, bringing with him a collection of vines made by the Scots viticulturist, James Busby, during a tour of the vineyards of France and Spain, but his tenure of the post was short. He joined, as botanist, an expedition which set off in 1835 to ascertain the course of the Darling River and, having wandered away from the main party in search of specimens, he became lost and was subsequently killed by Aborigines.

Allan Cunningham came back to the colony as his brother's successor in 1837, but the work of Colonial Botanist was not to his liking, particularly the burden of supervisory duties in the Sydney Botanic Garden. He resumed the 'more legitimate occupation' of collecting, although by now he was seriously ill with tuberculosis. In his last letter, addressed to Robert Brown, which is preserved among his papers in the British Museum (Natural History), he wrote on 16 May 1839:

Sir Thomas Livingston Mitchell.

throughout New South Wales, and particularly for his discovery of the Darling Downs, but his scientific work was also of the greatest importance. His name was given to the coniferous genus *Cunninghamia* by Robert Brown, as well as to Mount Allan and Mount Cunningham on the northern bank of the Lachlan.

Allan Cunningham had been generous in allowing Oxley's successor as Surveyor-General, Thomas Livingston Mitchell, access to the maps and reports of his explorations. Until he came to the colony in 1827, Mitchell had been a major on half-pay at Sandhurst, who saw no promotion prospects in a country at peace, despite his record of service in the Peninsular War. Born in Craigend in Stirlingshire in 1792, Mitchell had received a good education, had strong scientific interests, and was widely read in several foreign languages. He was also a gifted artist. During the Peninsular War, his surveying work had brought him to the notice of Sir George Murray, the Scots Quartermaster-General, who later became Secretary of State for the Colonies from 1828 to 1830. It was with Murray's support that Mitchell was appointed Assistant Surveyor-General of New South Wales in 1827.

The reaction of the Major's mother, Janet Mitchell, to the news of his appointment is contained in a letter to her son, dated 4 April 1817:

Your letter...has both astonished and distressed me very much...For my part it is going out of the world altogether. How you and Mrs Mitchell and children will stand a sea voyage of six months is past my comprehension. I am well informed the country is in a deplorable state—no money in it...no person was sure of their lives or property—no society but the refuse of mankind...I have always looked upon this place with horror and pitied the families that went there.

However, her son and his family survived the voyage to Australia, and in the following year, when Oxley died, Mitchell became his successor. He was to hold the post of Surveyor-General of New South Wales for the next twenty-seven years.

I am now exhausted in subject and literally in body, I therefore close, begging you, my dear sir, to receive this unconnected letter from the hand of a poor, decrepit, prematurely-old traveller who, if he did not do what he might with the means he possessed, formerly strove to advance, for years, botanic science here from pure love, blending the augmentation of our knowledge of the plants of the country with that of its internal geography.

Three weeks later, on 27 June 1839, the forty-eight-year-old Cunningham died. He is remembered for his explorations

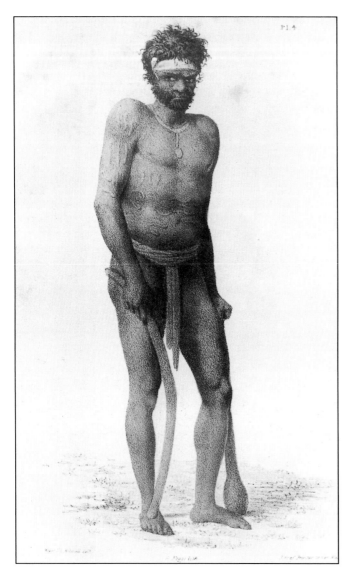

'Cambo', by Thomas Livingston Mitchell.

Mitchell found the Survey Department in a highly unsatisfactory condition, with insufficient qualified staff and a lack of proper instruments. Surveys had been made piecemeal, without any attempt to relate parts to a general survey; squatters were claiming unsurveyed land and disputes were proliferating. Realising that the development of the colony depended on bringing order to this situation, he set about the 'impossible task' of a general survey in 1828, laying out towns, roads and public reserves, and making personal surveys of the main southern and western roads in the colony with a view to their improvement. In 1834, he submitted to the Colonial Secretary a 'Map of the Nineteen Counties', detailing all the features of the various sections into which the colony was divided, with a recommendation that settlement beyond these areas be allowed only under strict control. The minute detail and accuracy of the 'Map' were much praised by Mitchell's contemporaries, and he himself described it to the 'Inquiry into the Surveyor-General's Department' of 1855 in the following terms:

I consider it one of the most accurate specimens of constructive plan drawing ever produced of an extensive territory on the same scale ... I have produced a map which will answer all practical purposes for which accurate maps can be required—and especially for determining general lines for railways or great roads.

Mitchell was keen to make a name for himself as an explorer, and he undertook his first journey into unknown territory in northern New South Wales in 1831. He went unsuccessfully in search of a large river which reportedly flowed towards the north-west, and reached the upper Darling River, but when his party came into conflict with Aborigines and two of his men were killed, the expedition was abandoned. In 1835, on his second expedition in New South Wales, Mitchell explored the course of the Darling and charted about three hundred miles of its length. The hostile Darling Aborigines who, as Mitchell wrote in his later account of the expedition, 'beset us as keenly and with as little remorse as wild beasts seek their prey', tried to check the white intruders and the exploring party was responsible for

The Murray, 27 May 1836, by Thomas Livingston Mitchell.

the death of several of their number. It was on this expedition that the botanist Richard Cunningham strayed from the main party, and Mitchell spent almost a fortnight searching for his fellow-countryman before it was accepted that he had met his death.

In March 1836 Mitchell left Sydney on his third expedition, to settle the question of the course of the Darling. As in all his explorations, he surveyed as he travelled, and in May reached the Murrumbidgee River. He followed it down to its junction with the Murray, and continued his journey to the meeting point of the Murray and Darling Rivers. The expedition then retraced its steps along the Murray and crossed it into an area of great beauty, which Mitchell clearly regarded with absolute delight:

Australian eagle, by Thomas Livingston Mitchell.

We had at length discovered a country ready for the immediate reception of civilized man . . . with an exuberant soil under a temperate climate; bounded by the sea-coast and mighty rivers, and watered abundantly by streams from lofty mountains; this highly interesting region lay before me with all its features new and untouched as they fell from the hand of the Creator! . . . it was indeed a sort of paradise to me . . . still unknown to the civilized world, but yet certain to become, at no distant date, of vast importance to a new people.

The description is given in Mitchell's account of his explorations, *Three Expeditions into the Interior of Eastern Australia* (1838), which also contained his own drawings and maps. His discovery, which he considered 'one of the finest regions upon earth', he named 'Australia Felix' – the Western district of the future state of Victoria – and its colonization, largely by Scots, rapidly followed. Mitchell's discovery of Australia Felix brought him fame. *Blackwood's Magazine*, reviewing his book in November 1838, referred to 'this gallant soldier, man of science, and man of accomplishment'. He also received a financial reward from the government of New South Wales and, even more to his satisfaction, a knighthood from Queen Victoria in 1839.

On his fourth expedition, in 1845, Mitchell went in search of a practicable overland route to the Gulf of Carpentaria, which would facilitate the trade in horses with India. During the journey he charted an extensive area of unknown land believing, wrongly as it transpired, that in the Barcoo he had found his great northern river. He published the details of this exploration in his *Journal of an Expedition into the Interior of Tropical Australia in Search of a Route from Sydney to the Gulf of Carpentaria* (1848), a work that confirmed his reputation as a great explorer.

Mitchell had a lively literary style, and was a man of wide interests in the arts and sciences. His other publications included *Notes on the Cultivation of the Vine and Olive* (1849); *The Australian Geography* (1850), for the use of schools; and a verse translation of *The Lusiad of Luis de Camoens* (1854), composed, as he explained in the preface, 'in a small clipper, during a voyage round Cape Horn' on his way back to Britain. In 1853, he read a paper to the Philosophical Society of New South Wales on his invention of a ship's propeller based on the boomerang principle, and published a pamphlet on the subject in London.

Mitchell was an assiduous worker, firm in the belief that all his waking hours should be spent in useful labour, but his official life was seldom tranquil. His nature was imperious and his temper short – he fought one of the last duels in Australia at the age of fifty-nine – and he was considered determinedly insubordinate by his colonial superiors, whose orders he occasionally ignored. They particularly disliked his habit of communicating with London direct, and of overstaying his leave in Britain. In the depression of the 1840s, the Survey Department was reduced in staff and in budget, leaving it inadequate in the face of the growing demand by immigrants for land. When Sir William Denison became Governor in 1855, he began an enquiry into Mitchell's work, and in the same year a Royal Commission was appointed to examine the Survey Department. Mitchell firmly believed its intention was to secure his dismissal, and anxiety, coupled with a chill, caught while out surveying, hastened his end. He died at his home, 'Carthona', in Sydney on 5 October 1855.

'I have been my own architect of gaining a noble name in Australia', Mitchell had written in a letter to Lady Audley on 31 August 1853. He is an outstanding figure in the development of Australia, for the excellence of his work in the Survey Department and for the explorations which helped to lift what he called, in the preface to the *Three Expeditions*, 'the veil of mystery' which hung over Australia. He was largely responsible for retaining Aboriginal place-names in Eastern Australia and, fittingly, his own name is perpetuated in roads, rivers, mountains and townships throughout the continent, as well as by several plant and animal species.

Another young man who left Scotland in search of wider opportunities was Dysart-born John McDouall Stuart, the son of an Army officer, who was born in 1815. He received some training in civil engineering at the Scottish Naval and Military Academy in Edinburgh, but, with his small stature and far from robust constitution, his father's career was closed to him. When he came to the new colony of South Australia in 1839, he obtained employment in the Survey Department in Adelaide, and it was probably from his work as a surveyor in the outback that he developed his taste for the lonely life of the bush, a taste he was to retain for the rest of his life.

In 1844, the explorer, Captain Charles Sturt, invited Stuart to join as draughtsman the expedition he was preparing to investigate the unknown interior of the continent. On this terrible seventeen-month journey through waterless desert, the party endured hunger, thirst, sickness and attack from hostile Aborigines. In the intense heat — Sturt recorded a shade temperature of 132° on one day — the skin was burned off the feet of the dogs, boxes fell to pieces and ink dried on the pen before a word could be written. Sturt's progress was eventually barred by the Simpson Desert and he came back, a broken man, his attempt to solve the riddle of the interior a failure. For Stuart,

John McDouall Stuart.

however, the expedition was an apprenticeship, a lesson which he was to put to good use in his own explorations.

Sturt's journey acted as a challenge to other explorers and, as a consequence, several expeditions left South Australia to explore northwards, including those by Stuart to Lake Torrens and Lake Eyre in 1858 and 1859, which were privately subscribed. Then, on 2 March 1860, Stuart set off with thirteen horses and two men on his first attempt to cross the continent from south to north. This was in response to the offer of a reward by the South Australian

'John McDouall Stuart planting the Union Jack on Central Mount Stuart, April 1860', by J. Macfarlane. *By permission of the National Library of Australia.*

government to the first person who could achieve this feat. After passing through the Macdonnell Ranges, Stuart made camp on 22 April 1860 near what he believed was the centre of the continent. Two miles away was a hill he named Central Mount Sturt, after his 'excellent and esteemed commander' (a name which was later changed by others to Central Mount Stuart). Stuart's *Journal* entry for that day read:

Today I find from my observations...that I am now camped in the centre of Australia...[on the hill] built a large cone of stones, in the centre of which placed a pole with the British flag nailed upon it.

In spite of illness the explorers went on, but scurvy, lack of water and harassment by hostile tribes forced them to turn back. Sick and exhausted, with their leader nearly blind, the party staggered back to Adelaide.

At the end of 1860, the government of South Australia agreed to finance Stuart's next attempt to cross the continent, and he left Adelaide early in 1861, three months after an ill-fated expedition led by the Irish-born explorer Robert O'Hara Burke (joined later by William John Wills) had left Melbourne with the same intent. Again Stuart was driven back by the waterless country, as he explained in his *Journal*:

There is not a mouthful of grass for the horses to eat...We are all nearly naked, the scrub has been so severe on our clothes...Our boots are also gone...The men are also failing and showing the effect of short rations.

Absolutely convinced that he could find a way across the continent, Stuart set off on a third attempt towards the end of October 1861, reaching the centre in March 1862. The party made painfully slow progress during what was to prove a lengthy period of drought, first through scrubland, then over marshland where they were tormented by ants, mosquitoes and sandflies as they floundered. As they went on the vegetation became more and more tropical, and Stuart realized that at last they were approaching the northern coast. Almost blind and badly afflicted with scurvy, he was yet able to write in his *Journal*:

Gratified and delighted to behold the waters of the Indian Ocean in the

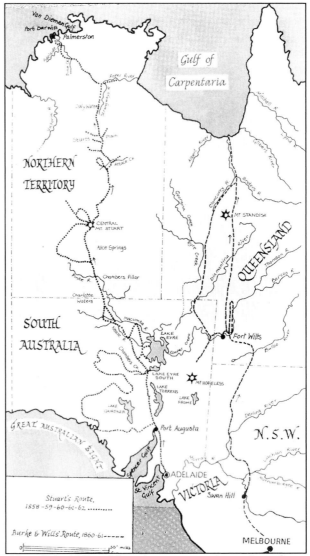

Map of John McDouall Stuart's route across the continent, from R. S. Clark. *Australia: Discovery and Exploration*. London, 1975. *By permission of Franklin Watts, Publishers.*

John McDouall Stuart's 'ambulance'. *By permission of the Royal Geographical Society of Australasia (SA Branch).*

Van Diemen's Gulf...the beach is covered with a soft blue mud...I dipped my feet and washed my face and hands in the sea...I had my initials cut on a large tree (J.M.D.S.)...Thus have I, through the instrumentality of the Divine Providence, been led to accomplish the great object of the expedition.

For both men and animals on the expedition, the four-month return journey was filled with distress, chiefly from want of water. Stuart himself was near to death, as he described:

While taking a drink of water, I was seized with a violent fit of vomiting blood and mucus, which lasted about five minutes, and has nearly killed me.

The gaunt skeleton of a man was carried the last 700 miles on a stretcher slung between four horses, enduring torments from this painful means of progress. The party reached Adelaide on 17 December 1862, having been away from the capital for a year and twelve days. Stuart had accomplished his mission — without the loss of a single human life — and he received a hero's welcome on his return.

On 21 January 1863, a public holiday was declared in Adelaide for the Great Stuart Demonstration held 'in honour of the gallant Scotchman'. Stuart and his companions wore their ragged bush clothes to ride through the town and receive the enthusiastic cheers of the dense crowds. The next day the *South Australian Advertiser* summed up the achievement:

The feat accomplished by the brave men is unparalleled...What was the map of Australia in our schooldays? What was it ten years ago? It was a vast blank, having no line traced upon it, no mark, even conjectural, by which an opinion might be formed of the nature of the vast interior...The interior of Australia was *unknown*. Was it a region of burning mountains, a desert of shifting sands...Was it a sea, or a lake, or a fruitful country? Stuart said *he would go and see*, and he went and returned to tell us.

On that same day the remains of Burke and Wills were being borne through the streets of Melbourne on their way to burial. They were actually the first to cross the continent from south to north, but they had died of starvation on their way back from the Gulf of Carpentaria. Stuart's great journey followed a more practicable route, and was saluted as an act of indomitable courage and tenacity, the *South Australian Advertiser* dubbing him 'the Napoleon of Explorers'.

Stuart had earlier been awarded a Gold Medal and gold watch by the Royal Geographical Society in London, and he was now granted the lease, rent-free, of 1,000 square miles of land in the North by the Government of South Australia. He tried to settle to a pastoral life but his constitution was fatally damaged by the privations he had endured. In search of better health, he travelled to London in 1864 and, while there, he placed his 'Journals' in the hands of a publisher. Edited by William Hardman, they were published in 1865 under the title *Explorations in Australia: the Journals of John McDouall Stuart*. The book was popular, and a second edition appeared five months later.

Controversy over the exact nature of Stuart's famous journey across the continent, and the faithfulness of his published account, unfairly clouded the final period of his life. Lonely, blind, and with a reputation as a heavy drinker, he died in London on 5 June 1866, at the early age of fifty. Only after his death were the facts of his journey and account confirmed. Through his explorations he had opened up a vast area for pastoral occupation, and when the Imperial Government later annexed the Northern Territory to South Australia, almost half a million square miles were added to the territory of that state. Several geographical features in South Australia and the Northern Territory were named after Stuart, but his true memorial was the Overland Telegraph from Adelaide to Darwin, which was constructed on the route he pioneered from sea to sea.

While Stuart was in the interior, news of the failure of Burke and Wills reached Adelaide and Melbourne, and

John McKinlay.

several relief expeditions were organized. John McKinlay (1819-1872), a native of Sandbank on the Clyde, who had emigrated to Australia in 1836 and had become an experienced bushman, was asked to lead the South Australian Burke Relief Expedition into the interior. He set off in August 1861, and on reaching Cooper's Creek, learned the fate of the missing explorers. Following his instructions, he then explored the country towards Central Mount Stuart and continued to the Gulf of Carpentaria. Since the ship which his party had hoped to board there had already sailed for Melbourne, McKinlay decided to make for Bowen, six hundred miles away on the eastern coast of Queensland. On

McKinlay Monument in Gawler, South Australia.

this perilous journey he and his men suffered extremely from the drought and the fierce heat, which also badly affected his animals. Almost the only food the explorers had was sun-dried horse and camel flesh, but under McKinlay's firm leadership Bowen was reached in August 1862.

Three years later, McKinlay was commissioned to lead an expedition to the Northern Territory to locate a site for development as a future capital. He explored the Liverpool, Roper and Victoria Rivers and discovered much good land. It was one of the wettest seasons ever known, and in June 1866 McKinlay was trapped by floods on the East Alligator River. A resourceful leader, he had the remainder of his horses slaughtered, had their hides stretched over a framework of branches, and in this makeshift raft the party set out on the attempt to drift down the river to the open sea. Drawn by the smell of the skins, alligators menaced the craft, which was nearly swamped on several occasions, but eventually the men reached a safe shore. On his return, McKinlay recommended Port Darwin as the best site for development.

McKinlay was an imposing figure, over six feet tall and 'upright as a poplar', with an exceptionally mild and gentle nature. He spent his later years farming in Gawler, South Australia, but, like John McDouall Stuart, his constitution had been damaged by the hardships he had endured, and he died in 1872. In recognition of his achievements in opening up Central Australia, the citizens of Gawler, where he was much loved, erected a fine monument of Aberdeen granite to his memory in the principal street of the town.

McKinlay's transport problems in the outback had been eased by the use of camels — animals which could go three times as far as horses without water. The idea of using camels in exploration came from Sir Thomas Elder (1818-1897), the son of a merchant and shipowner in Kirkcaldy. After emigrating to Australia, Elder had become a partner in a prominent wool-selling firm with enormous pastoral holdings, Elder & Smith. He had imported over a hundred breeding camels from India, with their Afghan handlers, to his station at Beltana in South Australia, and had there raised a stock of exceptionally sturdy animals. A hundred of them were used in the construction of the Overland Telegraph from Adelaide to Darwin in 1872, and camels came to be regarded as indispensable for the exploration of the interior.

The wealthy Elder was an enthusiastic promoter of exploration to open up new country, and he provided not only camels but the financial backing for several expeditions, including P. E. Warburton's 4,000-mile journey from the centre to the western coast of Australia in 1872-1873, Ernest Giles's explorations in 1875, and the Hon. David Wynford Carnegie's expedition across the desert between Coolgardie and the Kimberley diggings in 1896. Carnegie was the fourth son of the Earl of Southesk, and in 1892 arrived in Western Australia at the age of twenty-one to take up gold prospecting. The purpose of his expedition was to establish if a practicable stock-route existed between Coolgardie and the north, and he also searched for gold deposits on the way. With four men and nine camels, Carnegie kept a nearly northerly course through 'the great undulating desert of gravel' to his destination, and returned over endless sand dunes, a round trip of almost three thousand miles. He described his journey in a book, *Spinifex and Sand*, published in 1898, his only contribution to the literature of exploration. He left Australia in 1897 and went to work in Northern Nigeria, where at the age of twenty-nine he was killed by a poisoned arrow during a revolt in 1900.

By the end of the century, in the words of Ernest Favenc, explorer and author of *The Explorers of Australia* (1908), the 'stubborn conflict between the explorer and the inert forces of Nature' was virtually over —

It was by slow degrees, by careful study of the work of his predecessors in the field, and often by heeding the warning conveyed in their unhappy fate, that the Australian explorer added to the sum of knowledge of his country, and step by step unveiled the hidden mysteries of the continent.

Sir Thomas Elder, G.C.M.G.

'WE HAVE SEEN THE LAND, AND, BEHOLD, IT IS VERY GOOD'[1]

BETWEEN 1788 and 1900, almost a million and a half people left Britain and Ireland to settle in Australia, and of this number, it is calculated by Malcolm D. Prentis, in his book, *The Scots in Australia* (1983), that approximately 230,000 were of Scots origin. This outflow of Scottish emigrants, which rose and fell in response to changing economic conditions, continued throughout much of the 19th century, and had several causes.

In the years between 1780 and 1830, Scottish agriculture underwent a revolution. Greater knowledge and improved methods of husbandry brought more land under cultivation in a more efficient way, but the result was an increase in population throughout the country, an increase which could not be absorbed. Small village communities were disrupted by change and their inhabitants often forced to move to the newly-industrialized towns. In Edinburgh, for example, the population rose from 80,000 to over 150,000 in the first twenty-five years of the 19th century. From Glasgow, and other overcrowded urban centres, a stream of emigrants poured overseas.

In the Highlands, population growth had put even greater pressure on limited resources, as the old cattle-based economy was superseded by the more profitable sheep economy, controlled by large landowners and their agents. In the aftermath of the Highland Clearances, when by force or persuasion the people had been moved from their ancestral lands to make way for sheep, a considerable number of Highlanders had to emigrate in order to survive, though many left Scotland with the greatest reluctance.

Not everyone emigrated by compulsion. For men of substance, as well as for some of the poorer classes, the desire for economic advance was often a powerful motive, and many merchants, doctors, ministers and teachers, as well as artisans and agricultural workers, made their way to Australia in search of wider opportunities.

In the earliest years of the colony, many of the Scottish settlers entering New South Wales or Van Diemen's Land were men with capital, able to take up land and use it productively. Until 1820, they could only sail from southern ports in England, but in that year the *Skelton* became the first ship to sail direct from the port of Leith to Australia, with a party of emigrants on board. When he arrived at his destination, the captain of the vessel, James Dixon of Whitby, spent six weeks in Hobart in Van Diemen's Land and five months in Sydney, and he took the opportunity to travel about in New South Wales. On his return, he wrote a book, which was the first to appear in Scotland dealing specifically with Australia. *The Narrative of a Voyage to New South Wales and Van Diemen's Land . . . 1820*, published by the Edinburgh bookseller, John Anderson junior, in 1822, was an accurate and interesting account of the colony written by an eye-witness, and it was meant to help intending emigrants. Dixon was greatly impressed with Van Diemen's Land and considered that 'The Governor acts on the most liberal terms

1. Quotation (Judges 18.9) from the title-page of John Dunmore Lang's *An Historical and Statistical Account of New South Wales*. London, 1834.

'The Costume of the Australasians', 1817, by Sophia Campbell.

'Sydney in all its Glory', 1817, by Sophia Campbell.

with regard to [land] grants'. His conclusion was, 'If a man *can* live at home, let him do so. If he *must* emigrate, Australia is the best quarter he can choose'.

Commercial interest in Australia had been growing in Scotland, and in 1822 the Australian Company of Edinburgh and Leith was founded for trading purposes. The Company's *Prospectus* of 1822 emphasized the attractions of Australia as a land to settle in:

The fertility of the soil, the salubrity of the climate, the abundance of coal, lime and ironstone, timber etc ... and the advantages enjoyed by the colony from the suitableness of its Rivers and Harbours for Commerce ... make Australia the most suitable of all our Colonies for the reception of British settlers.

The Company offered passages to Australia at fifty guineas cabin or twenty-four guineas steerage, sailing directly from Leith, and between 1823 and 1831 carried 664 of the approximately 900 Scots who emigrated to Australia in Scottish vessels during that period. A Mr G. A. Robinson, for example, travelled out steerage on the *Triton* in 1823, and kept a journal of the voyage (now in the Mitchell Library, Sydney). He recorded that the steerage passengers were 'very comfortably off for food', and that the ship was well run, the captain conducting himself 'in every respect like a gentleman'.

Most of the passengers on the Company's ships were men with capital, but in order to make up the complement of steerage passengers, the Company was willing to give assistance to deserving masons, wrights, smiths and other artisans who wished to emigrate, either by a bond or indenture involving the repayment of a loan, or by selecting emigrants to suit the specified requirements of colonists. In the latter scheme, as the Company's advertisement in the

Hobart Town Gazette of 15 October 1824 explained, 'The Manager of the Company in Scotland will personally satisfy himself that the mechanics or others he may thus engage are of undoubted moral character... and for whose integrity and abilities he can pledge himself'. In the ten years of its existence, the Company played an important part in encouraging middle and lower class emigration, and in focusing the attention of the Scots on Australia.

One penniless Scot who went to make his fortune in Australia at this time was Philip Russell (1796-1844), who was born on his family's farm in Fife just before the turn of the century. He was brought up in the frugal, hard-working Presbyterian tradition, sharing the labour of the farm with his twelve brothers and sisters, and when his father lost all his savings and could not provide for his family, his sons were encouraged to think of a future overseas. Because of Philip Russell's experience of farming, he was offered the job of farm manager by a retired East India Company officer, who had acquired property in Van Diemen's Land. Before he left Scotland, Russell, on behalf of his new employer, engaged the skilled workers who would be needed on the new farm — two stonemasons, two carpenters, a blacksmith and a ploughman — and the group sailed from Leith in August 1821. Over the next nine years Russell prospered to the extent that in 1831 his younger brother George came out from Scotland to join him.

In the early years of emigration to Australia, Van Diemen's Land was a favourite destination of Scottish settlers, who were encouraged by favourable reports of the island, such as that contained in a letter from a settler printed in the *Edinburgh Evening Courant* of 23 November 1822:

Within the present year the population of these parts has much improved in respectability, and the order of the colonial officers, prohibiting the permission to settle here of any individual not possessing upwards of £500, has made it at once select and creditable, and has tended to improve the wealth of the place, as almost all settlers prefer this to any other part of New South Wales, both on account of its fertility and its general respectability.

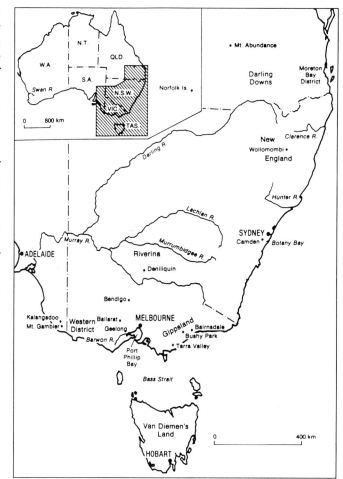

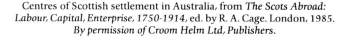

Centres of Scottish settlement in Australia, from *The Scots Abroad: Labour, Capital, Enterprise, 1750-1914*, ed. by R. A. Cage. London, 1985. *By permission of Croom Helm Ltd, Publishers.*

Between decks on an emigrant ship. *Illustrated London News*,
17 August 1850.

The *Scotsman* at this time published opinions unfavourable to the Australian colony, which was rejected as a field for emigration on the grounds of its distance from Britain, its lack of towns, the existence of the convict element in the population, and its 'despotic government'.

In order to meet Australia's need for population, the colony in the 1830s began to use the revenue generated by land sales to subsidize the passages of emigrants from Britain. Lower middle class and working class families in Scotland, who had not previously been able to afford the fares, were thus able to take advantage of the colonial bounty system, which from 1837 operated alongside government assisted schemes. A dramatic increase in the rate of emigration occurred. Only 114 people had left Scotland for Australia in 1836, but by 1837 the figure had increased to 1,254, and rose to a peak of 3,215 in 1838.

From 1836, the person responsible for selecting Scottish emigrants was Dr Charles Boyter, the 'Colonial Emigration Agent' in Scotland, who travelled thousands of miles throughout the country encouraging suitable emigrants to come forward. In the Highlands, opinion about Boyter's activities was divided. The *Inverness Courier* of 30 May 1838 reported his arrival in Fort William on the 18th in these terms:

The news of his arrival, like the fiery cross of old, soon spread through every glen of the district, and at an early hour on Monday, thousands of enterprising Gaels might be seen ranked around the Caledonian Hotel, anxious to quit the land of their forefathers and to go and possess the unbounded pastures of Australia ... While we regret that so many active men should feel it necessary to leave their own country, the Highlands will be considerably relieved of its overplus population.

C. Munro, a banker and sheep-farmer in Dingwall, whose heart was 'sickened' to see so many of his countrymen emigrate to Australia, wrote in a letter, which was later published in the *Sydney Herald* of 22 May 1839:

If Boyter were ridding the country of its scum, we should be obliged to him, but he is depriving us of the very flower of the land. I don't know one bad man he has taken from this country.

Boyter's policy was to select able-bodied emigrants who would not be a burden in the colonies, but his exclusion of those who wished to take relatives was deplored by the members of the Highland Relief Committees, such as John Bowie of the Edinburgh Committee, who visited the Highlands in the autumn of 1837. He pointed out, in a letter to the Colonial Secretary dated 2 November 1837, that 'many who are willing to go to Australia cannot comply with the regulations'. Boyter subsequently relaxed the rules, and by allowing elderly relatives and family groups to emigrate, he ensured that emigrants of good quality would come forward. Between 1837 and 1840, twenty ships sailed from Scottish ports, with approximately 5,263 bounty emigrants on board.

In the West Highlands and Islands, the population had continued to grow despite an economy which could not support that growth. As cattle-grazing declined, so that the Highlanders were no longer able to trade animals for oatmeal, they were forced to depend on the potato as their staple food. In 1846, the potato blight spread from Ireland, and in some areas its effects were even more devastating than in Ireland. No Highlanders suffered more than those in Skye, where starvation and destitution struck the 26,000 inhabitants, more than half of whom were landless.

Public sympathy for the plight of the Highlanders expressed itself in the establishment of relief committees locally and in the Lowland cities. Emigration came to be seen as the best solution to the problem, and in 1852 the Highland and Island Emigration Committee was established in London by the English civil servant, Sir Charles Edward Trevelyan, Assistant Secretary to the Treasury, whose wife was of Highland descent. Trevelyan dismissed the work of charities who sent emergency supplies of food to the Highlands and Islands as a 'useless palliative', and he wrote in a letter, dated 3 April 1852, to Thomas Fraser, Sheriff Substitute of the Isle of Skye, of –

the necessity of adopting a *final* measure of relief for the Western Highlands and Islands by transporting the surplus of the population to Australia. This community is *tortured* and *preyed upon* ... the 'patient'

Melbourne in 1840. *Australasian Sketcher,* 10 July 1875.

and 'loyal' Highlanders being tamed by the mistaken kindness of his friends into a *Professional Mendicant*.

Two Scots assisted Trevelyan in the work of the Society, Sir John McNeill, son of the Laird of Colonsay, Chairman of the Board of Supervision for the New Poor Law in Scotland, and Sir Thomas Murdoch, Chairman of the Colonial Land and Emigration Commissioners. Together, they drew up a plan of operations which would in general allow whole families to emigrate, with passages to be provided by the Commissioners from colonial funds, and money to be advanced by the Society for the emigrants to buy outfits. Landlords of the properties from which the emigrants departed would be expected to pay one third of the sum disbursed by the Society, and the emigrants themselves were required to repay their debt to the Society 'to the last penny'. The monies thus received were to be used to send out further emigrants.

The desperate condition of the people of Skye is revealed in a letter to Trevelyan from a Mr Chant, which was published in the *Report of the Highland Emigration Society, 1852-1853*. Chant was an experienced emigration officer, who visited the island in 1852:

I cannot conclude without referring to the destitution of the Island of Skye. It would be difficult, perhaps impossible, to convey to you an idea of the wretchedness and misery I have witnessed. *It must be seen to be understood*...It is not too much to say that many of the swine in England are better fed and better housed than are the poor of this island. The meal and buttermilk on which they are fattened would be received with thankfulness, and make the hearts of many poor creatures leap for joy.

With the help of Mr Chant, a group of 372 emigrants was quickly gathered by the Skye Committee and brought to the Clyde to board the *Georgiana*, bound for Melbourne. The scene at Greenock when the ship sailed on 13 July 1852 was described by a newspaper, the *Glasgow Constitutional*, four days later. The Reverend Dr Norman MacLeod of Glasgow spoke to the people in Gaelic —

at great length...the 23rd Psalm was sung, amidst much sobbing, and under very deep impressions...Not one bitter word was spoken against landlord or factor. They declared, in very touching language, that they went forth trusting in God, as did Abraham of old, not doubting that he was sent of God for purposes of good.

The London Committee had decided that each ship should carry a minister and, at Trevelyan's insistence, a library of 'solid and amusing books'. What could not be legislated for was the health of the passengers. When the *Hercules*, with 380 emigrants on board, sailed from Campbeltown in December of the same year, smallpox, followed by fever, broke out on board, and fifty-six people, including the surgeon and the matron, died.

In its *Report, 1852-1853*, the Highland and Island Emigration Society published some carefully selected letters sent by emigrants to their relatives in Skye. John McKinnon, aged 62, formerly a labourer, wrote:

Now, Sandy, it is no profit to me to tell you lies. That I will not. I heard at home good accounts of Australia; but I never believed it till I saw it with my own eyes...They do not care about a sovereign here more than you of a penny at home...I have in my possession this night, after clearing all my expenses, twenty pounds sterling...How long I would be in Skye before I would gather as much!...When I came ashore I had only 10/-.

Another letter was from Alexander Cameron, who emigrated on the *Georgiana* with his family of seven children:

I am a sheepheard here, at a man, John Gordon MacMillan, a native of Argyllshire...I have 3,000 sheeps before me. Ewen, my son, is with me, and Mary, Kenneth, and Sandy...our wages come to 75/-, our allowance come to 42lbs of mutton, 30lbs of flour, 6lbs of sugar, 3/4lb of tea; so there is plenty per week for ourselves and the two liddle boys.

Gratified by the results of his efforts, Trevelyan, in a letter to Sir John McNeill dated 31 July 1852, prophesied, 'Five hundred years hence, a few of the most aristocratic families of the great Australian Republic will boast of being able to trace their ancestors in the Highland Emigration Book of 1852-53'.

In 1852, the Society sent seventeen ships carrying 2,605 emigrants to Australia, and this was its most successful year.

'A real "Scottish Grievance"', from Donald Ross. *Real Scottish Grievances*. Glasgow, 1854.

As time went on, the Society's close association with Highland landlords, and its use of the landlords' factors, who, on occasion, used oppressive methods to organize the emigrants, was increasingly resented. In 1854, a Glasgow Advocate, Donald Ross, described the eviction of tenants from the Macdonald estates in Skye in a pamphlet, *Real Scottish Grievances*, published in Glasgow:

Lord Macdonald's ground officer, with a body of constables, arrived and proceeded to eject in the most heartless manner the whole population and that at a period when the able-bodied male members of the families were away from home...In spite of the wailing of the helpless women and children, the cruel work was proceeded with as rapidly as possible...No mercy was shown to age or sex, all were indiscriminately thrust out and left to perish on the hills.

Trevelyan had not achieved his aim of a 'final settlement' of the Highland problem by mass emigration, but between 1852 and 1857, under the Society's direction, twenty-nine ships carried 4,910 men, women and children from Skye, Harris, North Uist, Ardnamurchan, Morvern and the small islands to a new life in Australia. The largest number, 3,134, of the emigrants went to Victoria, and of the remainder, 848 went to South Australia, 537 to New South Wales, and 391 to Van Diemen's Land. The colonies needed labour, especially pastoral workers, and Trevelyan believed that Highlanders, accustomed to herding sheep and cattle, were highly suitable for such work. The Society's first emigrants arrived in Australia at a propitious time, when local workers were deserting their jobs in droves to go to the newly-discovered goldfields, but as the boom passed and the demand for labour lessened, work became harder to find. At the same time, the economy in Scotland began to recover, and the Highland people no longer had the stark choice of emigration or starvation. In 1857, therefore, the Highland and Island Emigration Society was disbanded, and its records lodged in Register House, Edinburgh. 'They may have some social and statistical interest hereafter', Trevelyan had written to Sir John McNeill on 16 November 1855.

The individual who did most to promote emigration from Scotland to Australia in the 19th century was the energetic and public-spirited Scots minister, Dr John Dunmore Lang. Born in Greenock in 1799, he was educated at the parish school in Largs and at the University of Glasgow, before being licensed to preach in 1820 by the Presbytery of Irvine. He was encouraged to emigrate by a brother who was already in Australia, and travelled there at his own expense, arriving in 1823. Soon afterwards, the Scots Church congregation in Sydney was established, and in 1826 the Church building was opened for worship, with Lang as its first minister. His career in the colony began as it was to continue, with a clash between him and officialdom in the person of the Governor, Sir Thomas Brisbane, on this occasion over official support for the Scots Church.

Lang was disgusted by the drunkenness and immorality he saw in the colony and, soon after his arrival, wrote in an unpublished journal:

The climate is delightful, the country is highly productive, but its people—O generation of vipers! Will they never be warned to flee from the wrath to come? I scorn to be the pensioner of thieves and adulterers.

John Dunmore Lang. *By permission of the Mitchell Library, State Library of New South Wales.*

The first week at sea.

Lang was convinced that the moral regeneration of a society which contained so many convicts and ex-convicts could only be achieved by attracting respectable and God-fearing immigrants, men and women who would bring new skills to the colony, and set a good example of sobriety and thrift. In Australia he saw a 'promised land' for the surplus population of Britain, and particularly of his native Scotland.

As a first step towards the improvement of the colony, Lang vigorously promoted the idea of building a Presbyterian college in Sydney, and in 1830 he travelled to Britain to place his plans before the authorities. He succeeded in obtaining a loan from the Colonial Office in London, part of which he used to charter a vessel in Greenock to take out the emigrants he needed to build and staff his college. He recruited fifty-four men of good character—masons, bricklayers, carpenters, joiners, plasterers and blacksmiths—and entered into a formal agreement with them. They were guaranteed work for twelve months after their arrival in the colony and, in turn, they agreed to repay Lang by regular weekly instalments from their wages. As well as the 'Scotch Mechanics' and their families, the *Stirling Castle* carried two ministers, three 'professors' for the college and Lang's eighteen-year-old cousin, Wilhelmina Mackie, whom he married during the voyage.

The grinding poverty Lang saw in England and Scotland during his visit in 1830 made a deep impression on him, and when he returned to Australia he campaigned even more vigorously for Protestant emigration from Britain as a solution to the problems of overpopulation and unemployment. By means of lectures, speeches at public meetings, and letters to the press, as well as in his own newspapers and in his large output of books and pamphlets, he pressed the case for emigration. An indefatigable traveller, Lang made nine voyages home between 1823 and 1874, and he travelled extensively, especially throughout Scotland, persuading his listeners to turn their thoughts from Canada and to emigrate to Australia. He was responsible for organizing several more emigrant ships from Scottish ports, to carry out destitute Highlanders, unemployed Lowland artisans and farm workers, as well as persons of independent means. In 1849, six shiploads of emigrants sailed, three to Moreton Bay and three to Port Phillip.

Lang used the long hours he spent at sea for literary work, and each of his voyages usually produced a book. His best known work, for long the standard history of Australia, was *An Historical and Statistical Account of New South Wales*, published in 1834, which ran to four editions. The title-page of the book bore a Biblical quotation from Judges 18.9: 'We have seen the land, and, behold, it is very good'. In the book, Lang wrote:

Let no cold-blooded political economist, therefore, presume to reason down the propriety of emigration, so as to deter virtuous and industrious families and individuals from adopting that expedient, or to prevent the British government from affording them encouragement and assistance. Let no affected patriotism throw any obstacles in the way of a measure that would enable thousands...to live in comfort and independence abroad, instead of struggling with increasing poverty and privations at home.

In all, Lang published nearly three hundred books and pamphlets, among them *Transportation and Colonization* (1837), two works, *Cooksland* (1847) and *Phillipsland* (1847), in which he recommended to emigrants the districts which later became the states of Queensland and Victoria, and *The Australian Emigrant's Manual* (1852), prepared for persons interested in the colony's goldfields. The rising number of Irish immigrants to Australia, as a consequence of the famine of the 1840s, drew from Lang a pamphlet, *Popery in Australia* (1847), in which he attacked Irish influence in the country and argued for increased Protestant immigration to counter it. The pamphlet also castigated certain Protestants – back-sliders among his clerical recruits to the colony, who were denounced as 'four Judas Iscariots and eight full-grown specimens of contemptible shuffling and drivelling sent out as ministers of the Church of Scotland in 1837'.

Lang was a man who 'sat hard to his purpose' and he made many enemies. His vindictiveness towards opponents was legendary. As a result, his public life was turbulent, and through his carelessness with money, and his recklessness with words, he received gaol sentences for debt and libel. He bombarded the Colonial Office with advice, and when his suggestions were ignored, concluded that it was 'staffed by fools and incapables – men who seem so utterly bereft of reason as if they had been indiscriminately taken from the cells of a mad house'. Yet for fifty years he dominated the colonial scene, as churchman, educator, politician, author and immigration organizer, and was the best known Scot in Australia. When he died in 1878, three thousand people took part in his funeral procession, which was the largest ever seen in Australia. A contemporary journalist wrote of him: 'Dr Lang has done more to advance the prosperity of this country than all other men put together'.

From the 1820s and 1830s onward, public interest in Australia as a field of emigration was stimulated by

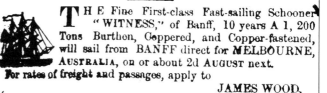

Advertisement for the *Witness*, sailing from Banff to Melbourne. *Aberdeen Journal*, 21 July 1852. *By permission of Aberdeen University Library.*

newspaper and periodical articles, by books on the subject, and by letters written home by Scottish emigrants. In 1827, a Dumfriesshire man, Peter Cunningham, who had worked as a surgeon on convict ships, and had lived in the colony, published *Two Years in New South Wales*. The book gave an optimistic account of 'our fine colony', and three editions appeared in 1827, followed later by German and French translations. In 1837, John Bowie's *Notes on Australia for Intending Emigrants* was published in Edinburgh, and in the following year there appeared *Three Years' Practical Experience of a Settler in New South Wales*, edited by John Waugh, and also published in Edinburgh. The book was made up of letters to Waugh from his son, David, a settler in the Goulburn district of New South Wales, which were written between 1834 and 1837. Since they were not meant to be published, the letters, which were full of interesting facts, gave an honest description of life in the colony, and the book was widely read. Eight editions appeared in 1838, and it received good reviews. Middle class emigrants, in particular, were reassured to learn that capital could easily be saved in the colony, land purchased, and convicts procured from the government to do the necessary work. Readers also noted that, according to Waugh, Presbyterian churches existed in country districts, and that there were 'a great many of our countrymen here, and all very clannish'. Another Edinburgh publication was J. G. Johnston's *The Truth* (1839), which reinforced what Waugh had said:

However strong his love of country, the man who prefers a dear farm and a life of unrequited toil amid the bleak, cold mountains of Caledonia to the certain and almost immediate prospects which this country holds out to him, cannot be under the guidance of reason.

In 1851, the news of the discovery of gold in Australia concentrated the attention of the world on the country. Gold was a powerful magnet to Scottish emigrants too, and one who decided to try his luck was a Mr Donald of Rubislaw, whose letter from Melbourne, dated 9 October 1851, to a friend was published in the *Aberdeen Journal* of 12 May 1852:

I think I will like this country well. The allowance for servants here is 10lbs beef or mutton, 10lbs flour, 2lbs sugar, 4ozs tea, a free house and fuel. Wages are from £26 to £30; but it is expected they will be higher soon, as the servants are almost all leaving for the gold diggings . . . I intend to go to one myself . . . Scotch servants are preferred above the others, the English next, and Paddy last of all . . . I would like to spend an evening among you all again: once I have dug gold enough, I will come and see you, and tell you some 'funny yarns'.

In the same issue of the *Aberdeen Journal*, there appeared another letter from 'the Land of Gold', written by a Turriff gardener, John Mackie, from Clare, South Australia, on 22 December 1851. The letter was addressed to Mackie's brother, Joseph, who was gardener at Delgaty Castle, Turriff, Aberdeenshire, and it began with an account of the voyage to Australia on the ship *Oregon*. The health of all on board had been good, and the passengers had been well looked after by the surgeon and captain, who 'maintained the greatest order and regularity at all times'. The letter continued:

I cannot omit here to mention the boiled beef soup, prepared by John Moir & Son, Aberdeen; it was served out to us three times a week, and was liked by all. I would advise all Scotchmen who have been used to oat meal to bring some with them for the voyage, as the quantity daily served to a mess of 8 would scarcely be sufficient for one brose to a single man, and it is often not good. We sold flour to the English for oat meal . . .

Mackie continued:

I will not advise you so long as you are in a permanent situation to leave all and come here; but I will give not my opinion merely, but the opinion of the oldest colonists that any working man or woman, of whatever trade or calling, and especially the labouring class, can do far better here than at home, and with one half the trouble and care too . . . I hope many more of our Aberdeenshire folk will come out—they will do well.

One working woman who emigrated alone to Australia in the early 1860s was Anna Allen, whose book, *Memories of My Life*, which was written in her sixties, was published in Adelaide in 1906. Anna Allen grew up in a poor family in Slamannan in Stirlingshire, and first went into service about 1850 in Denny, near Falkirk, when she was ten years old. Around the age of eighteen, when she was working in Glasgow, she applied to emigrate, and was accepted by the authorities, after she had produced a reference from her employers, and letters from her doctor and minister. Despite the fears of her family and the neighbours, who did not want her to go to 'that wild, outlandish place' where 'some thought I would get eaten', she sailed from Liverpool. On board the ship were other assisted emigrants:

Such a mixed lot of strangers I saw . . . There were Welsh and English married couples with their families . . . Then there were Scotch and Irish married couples . . . and single young Scotchmen, and single young Scotch women . . . There were 105 [single women].

Rough or fine, Anna 'never missed being in the open air for

'Off to Bendigo.'

one day during the voyage', which lasted for three months, and when the ship docked at Adelaide:

The head-gardener from Sir William Milne's [came aboard]... He had instructions to employ a young girl to do laundry work at Sunnyside, Glen Osmond, and he pointed out the place from the side of the ship under the hills. It looked so nice, and he told me they were a Scotch family...The captain, the doctor, and the matron were pleased, as there was a home found for me before I left the ship...Adelaide seemed a wonderful place. We admired the brightness of the sky...The very earth seemed new.

Sir William Milne was a prominent wine and spirit merchant, who had himself come to Australia as a farm servant in the 1830s. Anna enjoyed working in his 'well-appointed and happy home', and was delighted with 'the kindness of the people'. When she wrote home, she had good news to tell of Adelaide's prosperity, of the 'gas getting laid on in the streets...no unemployed...and no poor children without boots'. She was determined to bring her relatives out to Australia. 'There was a lot for me to do, as it would at least cost £20 for me to send the land grants to them'. In due course, her widowed father and younger brother and sister did come to join her.

Some years later, when Anna was visiting her former employer at Sunnyside, she was asked to help attend to some visitors:

I was told to bring in the decanter and cake to the library. There were two or three men there looking so weary and dusty. I learned while in the room that one of the men was John McDouall Stuart, the explorer.

A pioneer settlement in Victoria.

I hardly knew then what exploring meant. At any rate those men looked broken down, but the master was so pleased to see them.

Anna's later life was troubled. She rose in domestic service to become a cook, but made an unhappy marriage, and was subsequently deserted by her husband. She was 'left to struggle in bitterness all alone', finding 'the best balm for sorrow in a busy life'.

One Lowland emigrant who was a dedicated writer of letters to the newspapers was Andrew Carmichael of Pathhead, Kirkcaldy, an ironmonger and stationer, who emigrated to Victoria in 1855. At first he was a goldminer, and then he took up farming in Morphett Vale, and later Telowie, in South Australia. From the 1860s to the 1890s Carmichael sent a series of letters to the *Fife Advertiser* and the *Fife Free Press*, and in them gave news of the political, commercial and religious affairs of South Australia, interspersed with accounts of the doings of Scots from the Kirkcaldy area who had settled in the colony. He was a vivid writer, and captured for his readers in Scotland the flavour of colonial life. In one of his later letters, written in Adelaide on 1 January 1890, on the 35th anniversary of his landing in Melbourne, which appeared in the *Fife Advertiser* of 21 February 1890, he wrote:

Maybe some of your readers ask how we get on in Christmas holidays? even New Year. The former is a very hot day, scarcely a breath of wind, and when the glass is at 90° it is no joke. While your readers may have been starving with cold, ice, or snow, we were sweating at our roasts, puddings, etc under the shade as best we could ... [We] invited 1,100 of our waifs and stray children to a feast in the Town Hall on New Year's Eve which was a great success.

Carmichael went on to speak of a Mr J. Blyth, of Pathhead, 'who came out here some years ago with the late Captain J. Anderson, of Pathhead. He seems, with wife and large family, jogging away nicely'. He had also met a Mr William Weir, whose family was well known in Pathhead, who was 'still doing away at shipwright work, his wife and family are also helping to build up Australia'.

For some of Scotland's emigrants, the bright hopes of a better life in the new country ended soon after the last farewell was said, in fatal illness on board ship. This was the fate of the St Kilda emigrants of 1852. Thirty-six islanders, one third of the population, left in the *Priscilla* for Victoria, but sixteen died of fever on the voyage, and only twenty survived to reach Melbourne. For other emigrants, who arrived in the colony at times of economic depression, the struggle to live was as hard as it had been at home. But for a substantial number, Australia was a place of golden opportunity, where they could obtain land or employment which significantly improved their lot. For them, the last verse of 'The Captains', by the Australian poet, Henry Lawson, was true:

They found fresh worlds for crowded folk from cities old and worn,
They found the new great empty lands where Nations might be born;
They found new foods, they found new wealth, and newer ways to live,
Where sons might grow in strength and health, with all that God would give.

Christmas Day in Australia, from *Australia: a Popular Account.*
London, [1865].

'The Port of Leith, 1824', by Alexander Nasmyth (1758-1840).
By permission of the City of Edinburgh Museums and Art Galleries.

'THOSE WHO MAKE MONEY ARE GENERALLY SCOTCHMEN'[1]

IN June 1798, a young Scots entrepreneur named Robert Campbell (1769-1846), the youngest son of John Campbell, Writer to the Signet and 9th Laird of Ashfield, arrived in the penal colony of New South Wales to begin a commercial career which was to make him so prominent there that he was dubbed by his contemporaries 'the Father of Australian Commerce'. Campbell was born and brought up in the flourishing commercial seaport of Greenock, and at the age of twenty-seven he went out to India to join his elder brother in the family firm, Campbell, Clarke and Company, merchants of Calcutta. When, in 1798, one of the Company's vessels was wrecked on a voyage to Sydney, Campbell sailed there to deal with the consequences of the loss, and took the opportunity to investigate the colony's trading potential. Despite the existence of a group of officers and officials who closely controlled the import of goods into New South Wales, the Company decided that Campbell should represent it in Sydney, and in 1800 he settled in the town as its first 'free' merchant. He was allowed by the authorities to lease land on Sydney Cove, where he built a residence, warehouses, and a wharf – known as 'Campbell's Wharf'.

Acting under contract from the colonial government, Campbell was responsible for importing a considerable quantity of livestock from India between 1800 and 1803, and as a result the colony's depleted herds of cattle were doubled in size. His general commercial activities and his fair-trading practices were much appreciated by his fellow-settlers, and in 1804 two hundred of them expressed their gratitude to him in a Memorial which stated: 'But for you, we had still been a prey to the Mercenary, unsparing Hand of Avarice and Extortion'.

Campbell was the largest employer in the sealing and whaling business which, in the early days, provided the colony's chief exports, and in 1805 he sent the first large-scale shipment of seal oil and skins to London, in defiance of the East India Company's monopoly of the Australian trade. On arrival, the ship and its cargo were seized, and only the intervention of the influential Sir Joseph Banks saved Campbell from a disastrous financial loss. The venture did, however, help to end the Company's trading monopoly, and in 1815 Sydney was declared a free port, a decision which greatly promoted the colony's trade.

Campbell was a leading member of the group of merchants and officials which, with Governor Macquarie's encouragement, promoted the establishment of the colony's first bank, the Bank of New South Wales, in 1817. He was also the Secretary of the Savings Bank set up in 1819 to encourage thrift among 'the Industrious Poor of the Colony'. The Sydney branch of that bank was so closely associated with his name that it came to be known as 'Campbell's Bank'.

Soon after his arrival in New South Wales, Campbell had acquired land on the Hawkesbury River and, as his business prospered, he continued to extend his land-holdings. In 1825, he became one of the first settlers in the

---

1. Anthony Trollope. *Australia*. London, 1873.

Canberra district, building himself a fine stone residence there which he named 'Duntroon' after his ancestors' castle in Argyll. A man of high standing in the colonial community, Campbell served in the Legislative Council from 1825 until he retired from public life in 1843. He died at Duntroon in 1846. In the words of his biographer, Margaret Steven, in *Merchant Campbell* (1965): 'His career in Australia had been a triumph of commonsense. He was one of the few of his generation who, bringing his ambition and his initiative to the colony, was neither broken, deranged nor entirely embittered by his experiences'.

Another Scot who made his mark on the commercial life of the new colony was Fife-born Alexander Berry (1781-1873). After studying medicine at the Universities of St Andrews and Edinburgh, and working as a surgeon with the East India Company, Berry abandoned his medical career in favour of commerce. He settled in Sydney in 1819 and, with a partner, set up a general merchants' business in the town. He also obtained a grant of land near the Shoalhaven River, an estate which was over the years extended by purchase until it totalled 40,000 acres. There, using convict labour, Berry made handsome profits from the crops of maize, tobacco, wheat, barley and potatoes he sent to the Sydney market, as well as from the cedarwood cut on his property.

As a prominent merchant with long experience of colonial affairs, Berry, like Robert Campbell, was active in public life and served from 1828 to 1861 in the colony's Legislative Council. His private interests included the study of Aboriginal life and the geology of New South Wales, and he sent anthropological and mineral specimens from the colony to Edinburgh University Museum. In his later years Berry wrote his *Reminiscences* (unpublished until 1912), in which he briefly described his life in New South Wales, and emphasized its simplicity: 'When I am alone I always eat porridge and milk to breakfast . . . I eat it because I like it, for I am no anchorite, and like to live generously'. He was much distressed in his later years by the attacks of Dr John Dunmore Lang, who, on dubious grounds, accused him of 'heartless injustice' towards his assigned servants at Shoalhaven. He withdrew from public life and died in 1873 in his ninety-second year.

While the colony's commercial life was being developed by Robert Campbell, Alexander Berry and other Sydney merchants, interest in Australia was growing steadily in Scotland. During the 1820s, this interest was particularly strong amongst the merchants of Edinburgh and Leith, and in 1822 a group of them came together to launch the Australian Company of Edinburgh and Leith, the first public company in Britain to operate in Australia. Its leading figures were James Wyld of Gilston, a Leith shipowner and wine-merchant, Forrest Alexander of Oakfield, an Edinburgh leather merchant, and John Anderson of Gladswood, ironfounder of Leith. Of the ninety-two original partners, seventy lived in the Edinburgh/Leith area, and the rest in central or south-east Scotland. In their prospectus, the promoters indicated a twofold purpose in forming the Company—to restore Leith's importance as a trading port, and to open up a new market for their manufactures in Australia.

'The Leith Company', as it was known, flourished in its early years. Three ships were purchased and another, named *The City of Edinburgh*, was specially built at the Leith yard of Robert Menzies, one of the partners. The Company's headquarters in Scotland were at the inner harbour of Leith, while in the colony warehouses and offices, staffed by Scots sent out for the purpose, were opened in Sydney and Hobart. In the nine years of its existence, the Company exported to Australia a great variety of cargo, ranging from oatmeal, butter, salt, barrelled herrings, whisky, ale and imported wine to livestock, timber, and cotton and woollen textiles. Agricultural implements, such as sheep shears, winnowing machines and 'Wilkie's malleable iron ploughs' from John Anderson of Gladswood's Leith foundry were sent out, as well as barley, clover, corn and grass seed from the rich farmlands of East Lothian. One colonial newspaper, the *Hobart Town Gazette* of 9 April 1824, questioned the benefit of some of the Company's exports to a young Australian settler 'in his bark hut, barbarizing over one of the

The 'Philo Free' trial, October 1817, by Sophia Campbell.

Duntroon in the 1870s, by Marrianne Campbell.

Company's smoked hams, with a bottle of their best Bell's ale, a cup of their real Glenlivet whiskey... and one of the latest of Walter Scott's works'.

The greatest problem faced by the Company was the scarcity of return freights at a period before the wool trade was fully developed. Increasing competition from Greenock, London and Liverpool, and a glut of imports in the colony finally brought about its termination in 1831. The Company had been ahead of its time and, in Alexander Berry's words, 'had anticipated the progress of the colony by twenty years', but its lasting achievements had been to publicize Australia, especially in the east of Scotland, and to encourage the emigration of middle-class settlers to the colony.

In the 1830s, it was the merchants of the Aberdeen area who focused their attention on Australia, and the city became an important centre for colonial investment. In 1839, the

Benan (built 1875), wrecked at Cloate's Point, West Australia, in 1888.
By permission of the Ben Line Group.

North British Australasian Loan and Investment Company was formed, with J. F. Beattie, an Aberdeen land surveyor, as its manager in Sydney, but it soon got into difficulties. More successful was the Scottish Australian Investment Company, which was founded in the city in November 1840. Its 'Contract of Copartnery', printed in D. S. Macmillan's *The Debtor's War* (1960), emphasized 'the great returns obtained for the employment of Capital in Australia ... as compared to what can be obtained for it in Britain', and declared that 'The proper object and business of the Company shall be the acquisition of Land ... for Re-sale, or letting out for Agricultural or Grazing operations ... and also, the granting of Loans or Advances on the Mortgage of real property...'

Of the original 416 purchasers of shares at one pound each, the majority was from Aberdeen and the North-east of Scotland, and most were 'small people' who were investing their savings. The 'List of Shareholders' printed in Macmillan's book shows the democratic nature of Scottish investment at that time. Alexander McKenzie, Coachman of the North Defiance Coach, held thirty shares and Miss Easther Murray, Dressmaker, of Brechin, twenty, while a number of subscribers, such as William Scott, Tailor, Fetterangus, held as few as ten. A limited number of shareholders, such as George Taylor, Hosier, of Aberdeen, and Dr Robert Daun of Edinburgh, held as many as a thousand shares. The agents and cashiers of the Scottish Australian Investment Company were Alexander Stronach and Charles Grainger, Advocates, of Aberdeen, whose office became the headquarters of the Company. The name at the head of the list of the Board of Directors was that of Dr William Jack, Principal of King's College, Aberdeen.

As their Australian manager, the Scottish Australian Investment Company sent out Robert Archibald Morehead (c.1814-1886), son of the Episcopal Dean of Edinburgh, and he remained their manager until 1884. His shrewdness and business ability won him a prominent place in the colony's life, and ensured the success of the Company. Morehead's position was made difficult by the 12,000 mile distance between him and his Directors, which meant that letters could take almost six months to reach their destination. Stronach and Grainger sent him frequent instructions, which did not always take account of conditions in the colony, but Morehead attempted to keep them abreast of colonial affairs by sending them the Sydney newspapers. 'The most of them are trashy in the extreme', responded the Aberdeen Advocates on 21 December 1843, although they added that Dr John Dunmore Lang's newspaper, *The Observer*, was 'the only tolerable paper that we have seen emanate from the colony'.

Morehead had frequently to act on his own initiative, and in 1843, when the colony was experiencing an economic depression which lowered property prices to a ruinous level, he purchased a number of buildings in the heart of Sydney, as well as a key site on the town's waterfront, which he renamed the Bon Accord Wharf and Stores. He steered the Company safely through this time of difficulty, and on 16 July 1844 received an assurance from Grainger that the Board was 'satisfied that you have been most fortunate, most judicious, and most successful since you put foot in the Colony'. At first the Scottish Australian Investment Company was only a mortgage company, but under its Australian manager's wise and enterprising direction, its activities spread into wool, shipping and pastoral development, so that by 1846 it was one of the foremost businesses in the colony. After the discovery of gold in 1851, the profits from its property and pastoral interests in New South Wales greatly increased, and by 1866 it had also acquired Bowen Downs in central Queensland, for long the largest sheep and cattle station in the world.

By the mid-1830s, wool had become the staple product of the Australian colony. The first Spanish merinos had been introduced in 1796 and were used for breeding purposes, being later crossed with Saxon merino stock. The leading colonial farmer was an ex-officer, John Macarthur (1766-1834) of Camden, New South Wales, born in Plymouth of Scottish parents, who owned an agricultural establishment of over 60,000 acres. Through his efforts, the quality of colonial fleeces was greatly improved, and in 1822 he was awarded two gold medals for his wool by the Society of Arts in London. Macarthur was a most effective publicist for Australian wool and he successfully interested British wool buyers in the potential of the colony as a source of supply at a time when their market was expanding rapidly. In C. M. H. Clark's *Select Documents in Australian History* (1957), one merchant's comment is quoted: 'The climate [of Australia] has had the most extraordinary effect upon the fleece. Latterly they have been of varying qualities, but all possessing an extraordinary softness that the manufacturers here admire ...'

The expansion of sheep-farming in the colony in the 1830s was rapid and dramatic. Once the huge areas of pastureland that lay to the north, the west and the south of Sydney were opened up by explorers such as Allan Cunningham and Sir Thomas Mitchell, farmers and their

Stud sheep.

An old-time squatter.

owning, or able to borrow, a small amount of capital would buy a flock and overland it from the settled area through the sun-scorched plains, suffering hunger, drought and Aboriginal attacks until he found a suitable run. Some pioneers even brought their flocks across the Bass Strait from Van Diemen's Land, seeking bigger and better pastures in the Port Phillip district (later Victoria). Among these Vandiemonians were the Edinburgh-born Learmonth brothers, Thomas and Somerville, who were the first white men to see the area that now includes the city of Ballarat. They settled there on a station they named Ercildoune, after the family's Borders connexions, where they had 50,000 sheep grazing around 8,000 acres on their runs. The township of Buninyong grew up nearby to serve the needs of the settlers. 'What would the poor farmers at home think of having 150 and 300 square miles of excellent grazing or pasture land and agriculturalist land for £10 per annum?', wrote G. A. Robinson, Chief Protector of Aborigines, in his diary when he visited the area in 1840.

Another squatter in Victoria was Kirkcaldy-born Anne Drysdale (1792-1853), a middle-aged spinster who had farmed her own land in Scotland before emigrating for reasons of health. She arrived in Melbourne in 1840, and subsequently took up a 10,000 acre run near Geelong, on which she 'prospered exceedingly'. In her unpublished diary for 1844-45, Anne Drysdale described the day to day life of the station:

October   25:   Mr Dougherty called and promised to return in
                3 weeks to sort wool.

October   31:   Sheep washing: the last of the flock. Dry and fine...

November 1:   Shearing all day.

December 3:   Fine. Pressed 9 bales of wool.

December 8:   Finished packing 57 bales of wool.

The diary also recorded some of the difficulties of the squatter's life: 'All the sheep mentioned [as lost]...were got, but two days after, 47 were missing...these are all nearly got also, but a number have been bitten by the wild dogs [dingoes] and several have died in consequence'.

stock poured into the empty lands – to the Darling Downs, New England, the Riverina and Port Phillip. Since settlement beyond the area of original settlement – Mitchell's Nineteen Counties – was technically illegal, those who occupied the land without authority were called 'squatters'. Many prominent men became squatters, and in 1836 the government accepted the situation and allowed them to buy squatting licences for land in the unsettled districts for a mere ten pounds a year. By 1840, there were nearly 700 squatting stations in New South Wales, containing 1,200,000 sheep and 350,000 cattle.

There were many Scots among the pastoral pioneers who were drawn by the lure of 'new land further out'. A man

In 1841, Gideon Scott Lang (1819-1880), a native of Selkirk, also emigrated to Melbourne, along with his brothers Thomas, a doctor, and William, a farmer. They first acquired property on the Saltwater River near Melbourne, and then took up virgin land near Buninyong. A writer as well as a pastoralist, Lang in 1845 published *Land and Labour in Australia*, in which he proposed that a squatter should be allowed eight years of free occupation of his land, at the end of which he should be permitted to buy the proportion necessary to maintain his stock, the money gained to be used to assist immigration. In 1845 and 1846 he set off to look for good pastoral land, making long overland journeys accompanied by Aborigines, and thus became conversant with their ways. In 1865 he published another book, *The Aborigines of Australia*, in which he advocated firm but consistent treatment of the Aborigines, whom he believed should receive food from squatters who came to settle on their land. Despite such sentiments, it was clear that pastoralism developed at the expense of the Aborigines, who suffered displacement and sometimes death at the hands of the whites. As Weston Bate puts it in *Lucky City: the First Generation at Ballarat, 1851-1901* (1978), 'People who felt mastery over the earth were bound to treat them as irrelevant and expendable...The competing value systems of nomadic and sedentary societies met head on, and the former was smashed'.

One pioneer who made a remarkable journey in search of pastureland was Angus McMillan (1810-1865), a native of Skye, who came out to the colony at his own expense in 1838. He brought a letter of introduction to a fellow-islander, Captain Lachlan Macalister, who gave him employment as his station overseer at Camden, New South Wales, and helped to finance his exploration. In 1840, accompanied by Aboriginal guides, and using only a compass and one of Matthew Flinders' charts, McMillan followed the course of the River Tambo until he reached Lake Victoria. 'We had not even a tent, but used to camp out and make rough gunyahs wherever we remained for the night. [It was] a fearful journey over some of the worst description of country I ever saw',

McMillan wrote in a narrative of his journey, later published in *Letters from Victorian Pioneers*, edited by T. F. Bride (1899). He had discovered the 'beautiful rich open plains' of a region he named 'Caledonia Australis', but which was later renamed Gippsland in honour of Governor Gipps. McMillan established himself at Bushy Park, near Stratford, Victoria, and became a prominent local figure, briefly representing South Gippsland in the Victorian Legislative Assembly.

At first, many squatters lived in primitive conditions in bark huts on their properties, existing on a spartan diet of tea, mutton and damper (dough cooked in the ashes of a fire). They were often rough-looking figures, belted, booted and spurred, wearing blue flannel shirts and low-crowned cabbage-tree hats. As women began to join their menfolk in the bush, conditions improved for the squatters, although it was often a lonely and frightening life for wives, exposed to the depredations of bushrangers and Aborigines when their husbands were out on the runs. One Scotswoman who travelled from Van Diemen's Land in 1839 to join her husband up country near Buninyong, where the Learmonth brothers of Ercildoune were, at some distance, their neighbours, was Mrs K. W. Kirkland. In her *Life in the Bush*, published in *Chambers's Miscellany* in 1845, she recalled the achievements of her first two years in Victoria:

We had plastered the outside of our hut with mud...we had windows and good doors, and a little flower garden enclosed in front: we had built a good hut for our servants, a new store, a large dairy under ground, a new wool-shed, and had two large paddocks for wheat, potatoes etc, and we had now plenty of vegetables.

To celebrate New Year 1841 in the bush, Mrs Kirkland invited her bachelor neighbours to dinner, and despite the fact that it was a boiling hot day, gave them 'kangaroo soup, roasted turkey well-stuffed, a boiled leg of mutton, a parrot pie, potatoes and green peas; next, a plum pudding and strawberry tart, with plenty of cream'.

The shepherds who were employed on properties such as the Kirkland station were frequently Scottish, and theirs was a harsh and lonely life. Three men could be in charge of a

Ercildoune sheep station, Victoria.

thousand sheep, grazing over five miles of country in which the shepherds could be the only inhabitants. One man was usually the hut-keeper, who remained there all day, while the other two set off at daybreak in different directions with their flocks. A Scottish visitor to Australia, G. F. Davidson, noted in his book, *Trade and Travel in the Far East* (1846), that:

A shepherd on the hills of Scotland, who returns every night to his *bothie*, and finds a *warm* supper cooked for him by some kind female hand, is a prince compared to the exile of Australia, who comes home tired and sleepy at sun-down, and may then either chop wood to cook his meal, or go supperless to bed as suits his fancy...'

Good shepherds were in great demand in the colony, and their wages could be as much as thirty pounds a year with rations. Men who were fond of reading could find some solace in the bush, but others became 'eccentric' or 'dissipated and improvident'. Alexander Marjoribanks of Marjoribanks, whose *Travels in New South Wales* was published in 1847, reported the complaint of one outraged Port Phillip squatter, Dr Thomson, that shepherds' wages were so high that his men were 'drinking even champagne occasionally, as he himself had been offered a bottle of champagne by one of his own shepherds'.

As profits from the sale of wool brought prosperity to the squatters, they became an aristocracy of wealth and power, living in considerable style in their fine mansions. Anthony Trollope, who visited his son, a sheep station owner in New South Wales, in 1871, noted in his book *Australia* (1873): 'In the colonies those who make money are generally Scotchmen, and those who do not are mostly Irishmen'. The success of the squatters had largely been made possible by capital investment from England and Scotland which went to promote the development of the pastoral industry. Indeed, in the years between 1839 and 1850, the amount of Scottish capital invested in Australia was out of all proportion to Scotland's wealth and population.

Following the success of the Scottish Australian Investment Company of Aberdeen, other pastoral invest- ment companies came into existence, such as the Clyde

Shepherd's hut, from *Australia: a Popular Account*. London, [1865].

Company, a co-partnership formed in 1836, which was backed by a group of Glasgow merchants and landowners. Two of its partners were already settled on the River Clyde in Tasmania, but in 1839 they transferred their interests to Geelong in Victoria, and obtained a run extending to 20,000 acres. The Clyde Company continued successfully in business until 1858, largely due to the shrewdness and good judgment of its Australian manager, George Russell (1812- 1888), from Fife, who had emigrated in 1831. Russell was extremely methodical, and kept careful records of the Company's accounts and all his correspondence. These survived the passage of time intact and were published in seven volumes as *The Clyde Company Papers*, edited by P. L. Brown, between 1941 and 1971 — a remarkably complete record of a Scottish Company's operations at a formative time in Australia's history.

Another pastoral partnership was Niel Black and Company, formed in the 1830s. Gaelic-speaking Niel Black, who was born in Argyll in 1804, the son of a tenant farmer of the Duke of Argyll, was an experienced farmer when he joined William Steuart of Glenormiston, Peeblesshire, Alexander Struthers Finlay of Castle Toward, Argyll, and Thomas S. Gladstone in the partnership. He sailed to the colony in 1839, and after examining various areas, chose to settle in the Western District of Port Phillip (the 'Australia Felix' of Sir Thomas Mitchell) because, as he said in his Journal, it was 'a Scotch settlement'. He acquired a 44,000-acre run there, which he renamed Glenormiston, and under his direction the Company continued to acquire property until it was dissolved in 1869. Thereafter, Black farmed on his own account, giving employment to many Scottish Highlanders, and becoming a highly successful cattle-breeder.

Scottish investment in Australia continued throughout the 19th century. A writer in Blackwood's Magazine of October 1884 pointed out that 'three fourths of the foreign and colonial investment companies are of Scottish origin. If not actually located in Scotland, they have been hatched by Scotch-men, and work on Scottish models'. By 1875, the Bank of Scotland was acting as agent for the Bank of South Australia and the Australian and New Zealand Mortgage Company, and three years later it purchased New South Wales Government debentures, the first time it had made an investment outside the United Kingdom.

Among the ships which sailed between the Mother Country and the colony, carrying emigrants and manu-factured goods out and bringing back gold and wool, were numerous Scottish-built vessels. Some of the finest were owned by George Thompson of Aberdeen, who set up his Aberdeen Line in 1825. He entered the Australian trade in 1846 with his vessel the Neptune, and in the years that followed he provided a regular shipping service from London to the colony. Aberdeen and the Clyde were centres of great maritime activity in the 19th century, and Aberdeen in particular was world-famous in the construction of clippers — ships which, for faster sailing, were built longer and narrower than ordinary sailing ships. It was an Aberdeen Line clipper, the Phoenician, which, on 3 February 1852, after an eighty-three day voyage, carried the first consignment of Australian gold, worth £81,000, from Sydney to Plymouth.

The Company's most outstanding clipper was the Thermopylae, constructed by Walter Hood of Aberdeen for George Thompson. Two days after her launch, she was described by the Aberdeen Free Press of 20 August 1868 as 'probably the finest sailing vessel ever built in Aberdeen'. On her brilliant maiden voyage to Melbourne in 1868-1869, the Thermopylae, laden with a mixed cargo which included 923 iron rails, 30 tanks of malt and 265 cases of bottled beer, reached her destination in the astonishing time of sixty-two days. The news of her arrival was greeted with incredulity in Melbourne, as no ship had ever made the passage so swiftly, and crowds of citizens turned out to see her. Over the next ten years, her average time to Melbourne was sixty-seven days, and even when challenged by a famous rival wool-clipper, the Dumbarton-built Cutty Sark, her record remained intact. However, when the new triple-expansion engines invented by the Scot, Dr Alexander Kirk, were installed in the Aberdeen Line's pioneer steamship Aberdeen, built by Napier of Govan in 1880, that vessel's maiden voyage to Melbourne took only forty-one and a half days. The advent of steamships, and the opening of the Suez Canal in 1869, had rendered the clippers obsolete.

In 1875, the firm of McIlwraith, McEacharn and Company was founded by Malcolm Donald McEacharn (1852-1910), son of a sea captain from Islay, and Andrew McIlwraith (1844-1932), a shipowner's son from Ayr. The partnership's headquarters were in London, and the ships of their Scottish Line carried emigrants and cargo to Queensland. In 1876, McEacharn and McIlwraith paid a visit to Australia, where they both had relatives connected with the business, and they examined opportunities for expan-sion of their interests in the country. It was through their

The clipper *Thermopylae* photographed in Sydney Harbour, 1882.
By permission of Aberdeen Art Gallery and Museums.

efforts that, in 1880, the first consignment of frozen produce was sent back to Britain. The Clyde-built *Strathleven*, which carried refrigeration plant manufactured by Glasgow engineers on principles discovered by a Scot settled in Australia, James Harrison, successfully transported a cargo of frozen meat and butter from Australia. The venture was a triumph for the partners, and it opened the way to a great expansion in Australian exports to Britain, although at the time the partners lost money over it.

McIlwraith made several business trips to Australia, but still retained his base in Britain. McEacharn, who was a widower, came to Australia as managing director of the Australian branch of the firm in 1881, remarried, and bought pastoral property in Queensland. In 1887, as the emigrant

Shipping at Circular Quay, Sydney.

business declined, the Company formed links with another shipping firm, Burns, Philp, and opened an office in Melbourne, to which McEacharn moved. Thereafter, McIlwraith, McEacharn moved into the coastal shipping trade, carrying cargo and passengers to the new goldfields of Western Australia. McEacharn's business interests were varied and extensive, and he played a prominent part in Victorian public life, serving as Mayor of Melbourne from 1897 to 1900, after which he received a knighthood.

The firm of Burns, Philp was a purely Australian company, formed by two recently arrived Scots immigrants in 1875. James Burns (1846-1923) was born near Edinburgh into a wealthy family, and emigrated to Brisbane at the age of sixteen. His future partner, Robert Philp (1851-1922), came from Glasgow to Australia as a child. Burns made his money in retailing during the Queensland gold rush, and when he moved to Sydney in 1877 he left Philp in charge as manager of his Queensland interests. Soon afterwards he inaugurated the Queensland Steam Shipping Company, and in 1883 the firm of Burns, Philp was incorporated. It operated in the coastal shipping trade before extending into large-scale trade and shipping in New Guinea, the Pacific Islands and the East Indies.

Burns had many public interests, and from 1897 served as commander of the New South Wales Lancer Regiment and then of the 1st Brigade of the Australian Light Horse. From 1908 until his death in 1923, he was a member of the New South Wales Legislative Council. He is also remembered for promoting the establishment of the Burnside Homes for Scottish Orphans, at Gowan Brae, his property near Parramatta, New South Wales. Robert Philp too was active in political affairs, representing Townsville in the Queensland Legislative Assembly from 1886. In 1893 he became Secretary for Mines, and later Treasurer, and in December 1899 he finally became Premier of Queensland, serving until 1903, and again from 1907 to 1908.

By the second half of the 19th century, Australia was manufacturing many of her own goods, and Scots were prominent in a variety of these manufacturing industries,

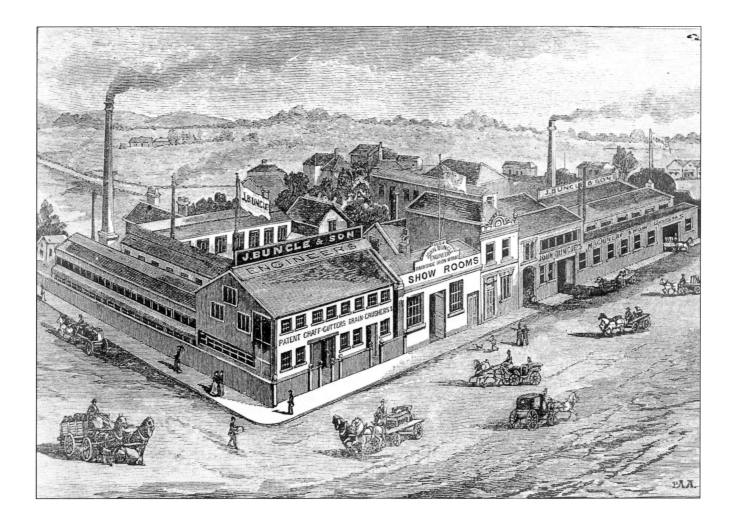

J. Buncle and Son's Parkside Ironworks, North Melbourne.

particularly in Victoria. Edinburgh-born John Buncle (1822-1889) was a locomotive engineer before he joined the gold rush to Victoria, and he eventually opened his own engineering works in North Melbourne. Robert McCracken (1815-1885) from Ayrshire began his brewing business in a small way, but by introducing scientific methods into the industry, he manufactured a light, bright-coloured 'colonial' beer which made him a wealthy man. The output of his famous City Brewery in Melbourne averaged almost 100,000 barrels a year. Hugh Dixson (1810-1880) from Edinburgh was the leading tobacco manufacturer in Sydney, while in the same city John Vicars (1821-1894) from Dunblane was the manager of a woollen mill which he subsequently took over, to become a leading tweed and woollen manufacturer. Sir Macpherson Robertson (1860-1945) was born in Ballarat, but learned his trade in Leith, and he rose from small beginnings to become a noted confectioner, conducting business under the trade name 'MacRobertson's'.

'THESE PEOPLE . . . GIVE THE PREVALENT TONE TO SOCIETY'

A VISITOR to Australia, writing in *Scribner's Magazine* of February 1892, observed that the influence of Scottish immigrants was very pronounced in proportion to their numbers in Australia. 'These people, the best of all British colonists, are found in all parts of the country, and in many towns – and conspicuously in Melbourne and Adelaide – control affairs and give the prevalent tone to society', he wrote.

The Scottish immigrants who came to settle in Australia brought with them the beliefs and traditions of their native land. The Presbyterians among them, led by a largely university-educated ministry, practised a religion which emphasized the virtues of piety, seriousness of purpose, and a sense of duty, and which, by its democratic structure, helped to encourage a sense of equality and an independence of spirit in its adherents. Scots of all classes also respected education and considered it an essential part of life, the means of 'getting on' and 'gaining an independence'. Many also believed that they acted as the instruments of God's will – Scots as different in background as Governor Brisbane and the explorer, John McDouall Stuart, conveyed this conviction frequently in their writings, and believed that, with Divine help, all obstacles could be overcome. 'The good providence of God and my own unaided exertions', the phrase used by John Dunmore Lang in a sermon preached in Sydney on Sunday 15 June 1823, soon after his arrival in the colony, expressed a commonly held attitude.

The first Presbyterian church in Australia was the little Ebenezer Church built in 1809 by a group of settlers at Portland Head on the Hawkesbury River, New South Wales. Services were conducted by a layman until John Dunmore Lang arrived in the colony and held the first communion service in the church in 1824. In that same year, Governor Brisbane laid the foundation stone of the Scots Church in Sydney, and on 16 July 1826 it was opened for worship – the first Presbyterian church to be built in an Australian town. On that day, the twenty-seven-year-old Lang (recently made a Doctor of Divinity by the University of Glasgow) entered the pulpit of the church where he was to minister, despite controversies and litigation, for the next fifty-two years, until his death in 1878.

Lang devoted his formidable energies to building up the Presbyterian Church, and brought out a number of ministers from Scotland to work in the colony. An early recruit was Glasgow-born Dr John McGarvie (1795-1853), who became the first Presbyterian minister at Ebenezer Church, although disagreements between the two men soon caused a rift. In 1826, McGarvie became one of the founders of the Sydney Dispensary (later the Sydney Infirmary and Dispensary), and was its honorary secretary from 1836 until his death in 1853.

It was from the nursery of New South Wales that one of Lang's immigrant ministers, the Reverend James Forbes (1813-1851) from Aberdeenshire, was appointed in 1838 to organize the Presbyterian Church in the Port Phillip district. He, too, appealed successfully to Scotland for ministers and by 1844, when the Presbytery of Melbourne was constituted and Forbes was elected Moderator, the congregation of Scots Church, Melbourne, had a fine Gothic building which seated

The first Presbyterian church.

500 worshippers, and ministers had been installed in Geelong, Portland Bay and several other areas.

As Lang pointed out in his book, *Port-Phillip* (1853), so many enterprising, middle-class Scots had emigrated to Victoria and established themselves as businessmen in the towns, or as pastoralists in the interior, that an influence had been created 'decidedly favourable both for its intellectual and for its moral advancement'. Many of the squatters gave staunch moral and financial support to the Presbyterian Church. One of them was Thomas Learmonth of Ercildoune who, conscious of the need for a minister to serve his newly-settled district, persuaded the Reverend Thomas Hastie, a native of Linlithgow, to settle at Buninyong in 1847. Learmonth, his neighbour, George Russell, and other Presbyterian squatters undertook to build Hastie a church and a manse, and guaranteed to pay his stipend of £150 per annum. They also promised to build a school in Buninyong—the first to be opened inland in the Port Phillip district. In the school prospectus, dated 1 June 1847, Learmonth indicated his motive: 'It is to be hoped that every district will, in the course of time, be supplied with Schools ... to train up an educated, industrious and orderly community'. For forty-four years, the Reverend Hastie worked at Buninyong, travelling great distances on horseback in the bush to serve his scattered parish. When he was at leisure, the minister liked to keep up his Hebrew, Greek, Latin and German by reading his Polyglot Bible every day.

The first Presbyterian minister had arrived in Van Diemen's Land in 1822, and a Presbytery was formed in 1835 during a visit by Lang to the island. In South Australia, Presbyterian services were first conducted in Adelaide in 1839 and in Queensland in 1849, but by then the problems which beset the Church of Scotland at home, and culminated in the Disruption of 1843, were being reflected in the colony and were causing serious rifts. By 1855, there were four Presbyterian churches in New South Wales alone – the Synod of Australia, with Established Church sympathies; the Synod of New South Wales, headed by Lang; the United Presbyterian Church; and the Synod of Eastern Australia.

John Dunmore Lang.

Moves towards unity began in the 1850s, but it was not until 1901 that the State churches formed a federal union as The Presbyterian Church of Australia. In 1977, the greater part of the Presbyterian Church united with the Methodist and Congregational Churches to form the present-day Uniting Church in Australia.

Religion and education were closely associated in the colony's early days. A short-lived 'Caledonian Academy', or primary school, had opened at the Scots Church, Sydney, in 1826, and within eighteen years the Synod of New South Wales was supervising thirteen primary schools in and

Scotch College, Melbourne, 1900. *By permission of the Royal Historical Society of Victoria.*

around Sydney, most of them with Scots teachers. In 1831, Lang's Australian College opened, staffed by three licentiates of the Church of Scotland recruited by Lang during his 1830 visit to Britain. In the twenty-three years of its fitful existence, the College educated over 500 boys in a broad range of subjects, and nurtured a generation of young men who later wielded influence in the colony's affairs.

One of Lang's 'professors' was Henry Carmichael (d. 1862), a graduate of St Andrews, and an educational philosopher, who for thirty years promoted the cause of education in the colony. 'My constant aim', he wrote in *The Australian* of 14 June 1836, 'is to facilitate, to the utmost of my power, the process enabling each mind to form, on all subjects (and on the subject of religion among the rest) opinions for itself'. Carmichael was particularly interested in the secularization of schools, and denounced Lang for his 'hateful bigotry'. He strongly supported the establishment of national, non-denominational education in Australia. Through his interest in adult education, he was also a leading figure in the foundation in 1833 of the Sydney Mechanics' School of Arts for the 'diffusion of scientific and other useful knowledge as extensively as possible throughout the colony of New South Wales'. Its first President was the Scots Surveyor-General, Thomas Mitchell, and Carmichael himself served as Vice-President for the first five years. The Mechanics' Institute movement, originally developed in Scotland, spread rapidly in Australia, supported by the work of Scots teachers and the benefactions of wealthy Scots philanthropists.

The divisions among the Presbyterians, and the fact that they were so scattered in Australia, in the end led many of them to support a system of free, compulsory and secular education provided by the government, and over the years many Scots teachers served in the national schools. A number of denominational schools continued in existence as private institutions – one of the most famous being the Melbourne Academy, or Scotch College, founded with the aid of a government loan by the Reverend James Forbes in 1851, and for many years the largest church college in Australia. Its Principal from 1857 to 1903 was the influential Alexander Morrison (1829-1903) from Edinkillie, Morayshire, who had been selected for the post by the Free Church's Colonial Committee on behalf of the Presbytery of Victoria. The Morrison family's involvement in Victorian education was considerable, for the Vice-Principal of Scotch College from 1869 to 1904 was Alexander Morrison's brother, Robert, and another brother, George Morrison, later became the first headmaster of Geelong College.

Alexander Morrison remodelled Scotch College on the lines of the school where he had been educated – Elgin Academy – and he altered the existing Classics-oriented curriculum to include modern languages, science and, for the first time in Australia, English literature. Scotch College provided education for the sons of wealthy squatters – the future leaders in every sphere of activity in Victoria – and 'The Ladies' College in connexion with the Presbyterian Church of Victoria', opened in 1875, did the same for their daughters. Similar colleges were founded in the 1890s under the aegis of the Presbyterian Church in New South Wales.

One daughter of a Scot who made a unique contribution to denominational education, and to Australian life in general, was Mary Helen McKillop (1842-1909), who was born in Melbourne, the daughter of an emigrant couple from Lochaber. Educated largely by her father, who had studied for the priesthood in Rome, Mary McKillop worked as a governess and teacher, but felt the call to a religious life. In association with Father Tenison-Woods, she founded, in 1866, at Penola, South Australia, a religious society named the Sisters of St Joseph of the Sacred Heart, which was devoted to the education and religious training of poor children in the outback. The Order grew in numbers, despite conflicts with the religious authorities. In 1875, Mother Mary of the Cross, as she became known, was elected Superior-General of the Sisterhood, and travelled widely in Europe, studying teaching methods. The Order continued to expand, and its schools, convents and charitable institutions spread throughout Australasia. When Mother Mary died in Sydney in 1909, there were almost 1,000 followers to

Mother Mary of the Cross. *By permission of the Mary MacKillop Research Centre, Sydney.*

continue her work. In 1973, her Cause was formally introduced by the Vatican Sacred Congregation for the Causes of the Saints, entitling her to be known as the Servant of God, Mother Mary of the Cross.

A Scot who contributed to intellectual life in the early days of settlement was William McGarvie (1810-1841), the brother of the Reverend John McGarvie, one of Lang's ministerial recruits. William McGarvie emigrated in 1826 and became the first professional bookseller in the colony. He had worked on the *Glasgow Herald* before leaving Scotland, and soon after his arrival, he bought the printing and stationery business of the late Robert Howe. Together with W. Stephens and F. Stokes, he founded in 1831 the *Sydney Morning Herald*, a weekly, which may have been named after the *Glasgow Herald*. In its first issue, dated 18 April 1831, McGarvie announced that the paper would promote the spread of knowledge and the advancement of education, and that its guiding principle would be 'reasoning founded on truth'. However, he only edited six issues before selling out to his partners.

In his bookselling business, McGarvie obtained his stock mainly from Edinburgh publishers — Archibald Constable, Robert Cadell, the publisher of Scott, John Anderson and Adam Black. On the evidence of his catalogues, he seems to have sold mainly books of discovery and exploration, series such as Anderson's *Edinburgh Classics*, Black's editions of Hume, Gibbon and Adam Smith, and the prose and poetry of Sir Walter Scott. Scott's works were very popular in the colony, and he was the only novelist represented in its first library, the Australian Subscription Library, established in 1826. The Library's first President was the Scottish Colonial Secretary, Alexander Macleay (1767-1848), who also made notable contributions to knowledge of the colony's entomology.

Admiration for the writer prompted one settler in Sydney to write to Sir Walter Scott informing him that he had named his property 'Abbotsford', and that he would 'feel great pleasure in sending you a Brace of Black Swans, Emus or Kangaroos, either of which I can procure for you'. Later,

Emus.

when news of Mr Harper's arrival in Britain with the emus reached Scott, he was appalled to discover their size, and wrote for help to his publisher on 12 July 1827:

My dear Sir

I am in a great & rather uncommon scrape out of which you must help me. One Mr Harper who went as a settler (not at government expence) to New South Wales thinking himself more obliged to me than perhaps he really was has brought over two Emusses for my special use and acceptance. Now I knew [no] more what an Emuss was like than what a phoenix was like but supposed them some sort of large parrots & thought they would hang well enough in the hall amongst the armour. But they prove to be six feet high and being as I take it akin to your ostrich may be cursedly mischievous besides expense & trouble. In this dilemma & not willing to affront a good & kind man I have written to Mr Somerville writer Edin^r (Mr Harpers friend) to get his permission to transfer the birds to the King and [if] Mr Harper will give his consent I would wish them sent with every due precaution by the next steamboat to the Royal Menagerie at the tower. Do for gods sake seek out Mr Somerville without loss of time and try to get me free of the Emusses; the matter is pressing for I expect every moment to see the Emusses arrive here followed by the whole mob of Melrose and Darnick.

If Mr Harper on my declining to accept them chuses to part with them at Exeter Change (which I should think a very sensible thing) he will get a very considerable sum for them. So that I shall not make my offer to the King through Sir William Knighton till I hear from you.

Yours in haste and tribulation

Walter Scott

12 July Abbotsford

[1827]

Of course I will be desirous to save Mr Somerville & Mr Harper all further trouble or expence with the creatures which is one reason of my troubling you.

For Robert Cadell Esq
Bookseller
St Andw Square
Edinburgh

Letter of Sir Walter Scott to Robert Cadell, 12 July 1827.

The fate of the birds, which were, according to Mr Harper, 'as inoffensive as Turkies', remains a mystery.

The pioneer educationalist, Dr John Dunmore Lang, had a strong interest in books and libraries, and established one of the earliest institutional libraries for the use of his students in the Australian College in Sydney. He also had a private library – 'my noble library', as he described it in a letter to the *British Banner* of 26 September 1849 – part of which had to be sold in 1846 when Lang got into financial difficulties. Of the 636 books auctioned, 300 were on church history and theology, 120 were books on travel, biography and history, and the remaining 216 were general literature (including a first edition of Cervantes, dated 1613), science, jurisprudence and philosophy, with the works of the Scottish philosophers being strongly represented. In the same letter, Lang reported that the sale of the books brought him £300, 'but I have a pretty good library yet'.

British interests dominated the publishing business in Australia until, in 1856, Glasgow-born George Robertson (1825-1898) issued in Melbourne a book entitled *The*

Discovery and Settlement of Port Phillip by James Bonwick, 'published for the author'. In 1882, Robertson took into his employ in his Sydney branch another George Robertson (1860-1933), who had trained in Glasgow with James MacLehose, bookseller to the University of Glasgow, before emigrating to New Zealand and then to Australia. The younger Robertson went into partnership with another emigrant Scot, David Mackenzie Angus, in 1886, and soon Angus & Robertson became Sydney's best-known bookshop. The firm also became publishers. Largely through Robertson's judgment and discrimination in seeking out and encouraging Australian authors, and his faith in the future of Australian books, Angus & Robertson played a unique part in encouraging the growth of an Australian national spirit. In its most illustrious period, the firm published classics such as Andrew Barton Paterson's *The Man from Snowy River and Other Verses* (1895), and C. J. Dennis's *Songs of a Sentimental Bloke* (1915). The long list of writers whose works were published by Angus & Robertson includes Victor Daley, Henry Lawson, Norman Lindsay, Mary Gilmore and Frank Clune. It was appropriate that for its trademark the firm adopted a thistle joined to a waratah – the crimson floral emblem of New South Wales.

A dominant figure in the world of publishing, Robertson was highly regarded in Australian literary circles, and was known as 'The Chief' by Henry Lawson, Australia's most noted author. Robertson could be dour with aspiring authors: on one occasion, he rejected a manuscript with the words: 'Dear Sir—Your stories are quite hopeless...give it up and take to gardening, or something else that's useful'. To Harry Lauder, the Scots entertainer, who enquired if Robertson would publish a book he had written, *Between You and Me*, the publisher sent the painfully blunt reply: 'We could not read the book'.

Robertson's special interest was Australiana, and in that field one of his biggest customers was David Scott Mitchell (1836-1907), the only son of a Fife-born physician and industrialist in the colony. Mitchell, a recluse, devoted his inherited wealth to forming, with Robertson's assistance, a unique collection of books, manuscripts, maps, coins and medals relating to Australasia and the Pacific. In 1901, with Robertson's encouragement, Mitchell made a will bequeathing his 61,000 volume collection to the then Public Library of New South Wales. The books formed the basis of the Mitchell Library, one of the world's most significant national collections, housed in the State Library of New South Wales.

Scots philanthropists were notable benefactors of the universities which had been founded in Melbourne (1850), Sydney (1853) and Adelaide (1874). One was a leading figure in Presbyterian circles in Victoria, Francis Ormond (1829-1889) from Aberdeen, who frequently stated that education was his 'ruling passion'. Ormond had worked as a boy on his father's sheep station at Mopiamnum, and was proud of having risen from stable-boy to wealthy pastoralist. His generosity to education at all levels was without parallel in Victoria: between 1877 and 1881 he donated more than £100,000 to Ormond College, a Presbyterian theological hall in the University of Melbourne, which was named in his honour, and he also endowed a Chair of Music at the University. He encouraged the foundation of, and contributed liberally to, the Working Men's College (later Melbourne Technical School), which was opened in the city in 1887. When he died, Ormond, whose name was a household word in Victoria, left an estate of nearly two million pounds, and many educational, charitable and religious institutions benefited from his will. The Commission of the General Assembly of the Presbyterian Church of Victoria, on hearing of his death, unanimously agreed the following Minute:

The Commission...desires, while humbly acknowledging the hand of God, and bowing to His sovereign appointment, to place on record an expression of their sense of the great loss which the Church has sustained in the removal of their esteemed brother.

In South Australia, Kirkcaldy-born Sir Thomas Elder, the wealthy pastoralist who introduced camels into Australia, owned an area of land larger than his native Scotland. He was a partner in Elder, Smith and Company, one of the

Ormond College.

world's largest wool-selling firms, and his philanthropy was everywhere apparent in the state. The University of Adelaide, in particular, benefited from his gifts. Twenty thousand pounds was given in 1874 to establish Chairs of Mathematics and of General Science, followed by £80,000 for medical and music schools over the period 1883 to 1897. On his death, the bachelor Elder, who had been appointed KCMG and GCMG, left large sums for the Adelaide Art Gallery and for Working Men's Homes, as well as bequeathing money to the Presbyterian, Anglican and Methodist Churches in Australia. In New South Wales, Sir Peter Nicol Russell (1816-1905) from Fife was a successful Sydney engineer and ironfounder, who gained his fortune supplying tools to gold diggers and machinery to the mining industry. In 1896, Russell gave £50,000 to the University of Sydney to found an engineering school, and in 1904 he followed this up with a further £50,000 to promote the teaching of engineering.

Many Scottish university teachers put their intellectual gifts at the service of Australian universities and influenced their growth and development. Scots professors were most numerous at the University of Sydney, and included Professor John Smith (1821-1885), the son of an Aberdeenshire blacksmith, who became the first Professor of Chemistry and Experimental Physics in 1852, and played a leading part in Australia's scientific advance. Smith had a particular interest in photography, and took pioneer photographs in the 1850s which have survived to form a unique record of contemporary life in the colony. Sir Mungo MacCallum (1854-1942) from Glasgow was the foundation Professor of Modern Language and Literature at the same University from 1887 to 1920. During his long tenure, MacCallum, with his 'scrubby beard and moustache...and broad Scotch accent', as one of his students, A. H. Chisholm described him, became an institution in the University. Dumfries-born Sir T. P. Anderson Stuart (1856-1920) became Professor of Anatomy and Physiology in 1883 at the newly-founded Medical School within the University of Sydney; and Louisa Macdonald (1858-1949) from Arbroath emigrated in 1892 to take up the post of first Principal of the

Francis Ormond.

non-denominational Women's College founded at the University of Sydney, an influential position which she held for twenty-seven years. Despite the preponderance of Scottish settlers in Victoria, Scottish academics were not so numerous at the University of Melbourne, although a

David Syme.

journalist and philosopher from Edinburgh, Henry Laurie (1837-1922), was appointed to the first Chair of Mental and Moral Philosophy at the University in 1881.

At the centre of Sydney's literary and cultural life in the 1850s and 1860s was the unusual figure of Nicol Drysdale Stenhouse (1806-1873), a Writer to the Signet from Coldstream, who had practised law in Edinburgh before emigrating in 1839 to Sydney in search of wider opportunities. Although not a wealthy man, Stenhouse had been acquainted with many of the major literary figures of post-Enlightenment Edinburgh, such as Christopher North and Thomas De Quincey, and in the colony he acted as a literary patron and as a link between the old culture and the new. His house at Balmain became a cultural centre for intellectuals, to whom Stenhouse made available his fine library of around 4,000 books. He also encouraged the spread of knowledge by acting as President of the School of Arts from 1867 to 1873, and simultaneously as a trustee of the Sydney Free Public Library. The Stenhouse library is now in the Fisher Library of the University of Sydney.

Several Scots played an influential part in the establishment and development of the press in Australia. James Harrison (1816-1893), journalist and pioneer of meat preserving, began his career on the *Port Phillip Patriot*, and in 1840 founded the *Geelong Advertiser*, which he edited till the early 1860s. Aberdeen-born Angus Mackay (1824-1886), formerly a pupil and then a teacher at Lang's Australian College, purchased the *Bendigo Advertiser* in 1855, and later helped to found the *Sydney Daily Telegraph* in 1879. Lauchlan Mackinnon (1817-1888) from Skye became a partner in the Melbourne *Argus* in 1852, and by his financial skill put it on a sound commercial basis. The most interesting figure was perhaps David Syme (1827-1908) of North Berwick, a man of wide education, who spent three years as a digger on the Victorian goldfields before buying a half-share of his brother's newspaper, the Melbourne *Age*, which first appeared in 1854. Syme took sole control after his brother's death in 1860, and for the next forty-nine years edited and published the *Age*, using it to promote a variety of liberal and radical policies which included free compulsory secular education, the opening of land for small farmers, protection for local industries and better conditions for workers. The circulation of the paper climbed rapidly, and Syme was able to wield a strong influence on political affairs. He wrote very little for the newspaper, but published works on government, political economy and Darwinism, as well as a philosophical study, *The Soul: a Study and an Argument* (1903).

The contribution of Scots to the literature of Australia occasionally showed the influence of their heritage, an influence which is perhaps most noticeable in the work of the poets who celebrated in ballad form the freedom and excitement of life in the bush. The most popular of these bush-balladists was Andrew Barton Paterson (1864-1941), the son of a Scottish grazier, who called himself 'The Banjo' after a favourite racehorse. Paterson spent his childhood on a station near Yass, mixing with teamsters and drovers, characters who later filled the pages of his poetry. In 1895, the publication of *The Man from Snowy River and Other Verses*, his first collection, made him a celebrity. The title poem, which tells the story of a heroic chase after a valuable colt which has escaped and joined the wild bush horses, has become part of Australian legend, and Paterson's book became the most successful volume of verse ever published in Australia. The poet went on to write many more volumes of poetry and fiction, which are akin to the work of Robert Louis Stevenson in their love of freedom and the outdoor life. He is probably best remembered for his famous poem, 'Waltzing Matilda', composed in Queensland in 1895. (Another famous Australian song had a Scottish origin, for Peter Dodds McCormick (?1834-1916) from Port Glasgow composed 'Advance Australia Fair', which became the Australian national anthem in 1984. It was first played at a St Andrew's Day concert in Sydney in 1878.)

A Scot who came to Australia at the age of twenty, and spent twelve years, from 1889 to 1901, working in the bush, was Will Ogilvie (1869-1963), a native of Kelso, who had been educated at Fettes College in Edinburgh. Drawn by his love of adventure, Ogilvie led a nomadic existence on remote stations, droving, mustering and breaking-in horses, feeling a companionship with 'the browsers, the biters, the barkers, the hairy coats' as he composed ballads and lyrical verse describing outback life. His best-known volume of verse, *Fair*

Andrew Barton Paterson. *By permission of the National Library of Australia.*

113

Girls and Gray Horses, was published in 1898, and contained a much-quoted poem, 'The Bush, My Love', part of which reads:

> The loves of earth grow olden
> Or kneel at some new shrine;
> Her locks are always golden—
> This brave Bush-Love of mine;
> And for her star-lit beauty,
> And for her dawns dew-pearled,
> Her name in love and duty
> I guard against the world.

The memory of the Australian bush remained with Will Ogilvie after he returned to Scotland, and it inspired much of his later poetry, as well as his volume of reminiscences, *My Life in the Open* (1908).

Ogilvie's work influenced another Australian poet, John Shaw Neilson (1872-1942), who was born at Penola, South Australia, the son of a debt-ridden Scottish immigrant, John Neilson, and his wife, Margaret Mackinnon. The poet's Gaelic home background, and his reading of Burns and the Bible as a boy, coloured his imagination when he began to write poetry in his teens. Despite a life of poverty and toil as a farmhand, roadmender and itinerant labourer, Shaw Neilson retained his gentleness and humanity, and composed a great number of poems, which he carefully copied into school exercise books. About half of these poems were destroyed in 1917, when a plague of mice occurred in the Mallee where he was living. His first poem to be published, in 1901, 'Sheedy was Dying', begins:

> Grey as a rising ghost,
> Helpless and dumb;
> This he had feared the most—
> Now it had come:
> Through the tent door,
> Mocking, defying,
> The Thirsty Land lay,
> —And Sheedy was dying!

A first volume, *Heart of Spring,* came out in 1919, and several more collections followed. At his best, John Shaw Neilson transcended his rough background to write poems of great delicacy, warmth and subtlety, which are said to contain Gaelic resonances.

From the earliest days, Scots in the colony met together informally to exchange news and celebrate traditional festivals, but records of early Scottish societies in New South Wales have not survived. It is known that on 25 November 1823 the members of the St Andrew's Club in Sydney held an anniversary ball, to which they invited John Dunmore Lang. His reply took the form of a humorous poem, included in *Sacred and Secular Poems Written Chiefly at Sea* (1873), which began:

> Friends of St Andrew and the Thistle,
> Accept, I pray, this short epistle,
> In answer to your invitation
> To the Grand Ball and Cold Collation.
>
> I wish you well as well may be,
> Long may you live in harmony,
> And every year in hot November
> The Caledonian Saint remember!

It was not until the 1850s, as emigrants poured into Victoria after the discovery of gold, that the first documented Caledonian societies began to appear – the Commun Na Feinne (Fingal Society) of Geelong in 1856, the Highland Society of Maryborough in 1857, and the Caledonian Society of Victoria in 1858. In an address to the founding meeting of the latter, the Honourable Thomas McCombie, a member of the Legislative Council of Victoria, who had been in Australia for sixteen years, said that in his experience the Scots were the most industrious, most independent and most successful members of the pastoral and business communities of the country. He asked the audience to do their utmost to promote the interests of their new country, without forgetting the land they came from. Another speaker urged the Society to promote the music and literature of Scotland and its national games in Victoria. In that same year, the

Members of the Pipes and Drums of the 1st Regiment, New South Wales Scottish Rifles, attending the 1908 Forbes Highland Gathering. *By permission of Martin J. Buckley, Esq.*

Caledonian Society of Ballarat was formed, followed in 1859 by a similar society in Bendigo. In a lively watercolour, the painter George Lacy captured the scene at 'The First Gathering of the Bendigo Caledonian Society, Jan. 2, 1860'.

The first Caledonian Society of Victoria did not flourish, and it was reconstituted in 1884 as the Caledonian Society of Melbourne (later the prefix 'Royal' was added). Its membership rose to 288 by the end of the first year, and several prominent figures in Victoria, such as the philanthropist, Francis Ormond, and the journalists David Syme and Lauchlan Mackinnon, also joined. The Society agreed that its aims should be to help Scots who were in distress because of illness or unemployment (or their widows), to

Dame Nellie Melba, 1904. *By permission of the National Portrait Gallery.*

give assistance to Scots newly arrived in the colony, and to promote the Society by means of sports meetings and social gatherings. At their first St Andrew's Day Dinner in 1884, the Society's Patron, the popular and respected Governor of Victoria, Sir Henry Loch (1827-1900) from Edinburgh, was the principal speaker. 'Scots generally succeed in any path of life they may enter', he told them. The long toast list of the evening began with the loyal toast, and came to an end with 'The Land o' Cakes' and 'The Land of Our Adoption'. The Society grew steadily, organizing sports, concerts and Caledonian balls for its members, and in 1890 the new Scottish Governor of Victoria, the 7th Earl of Hopetoun (1860-1908), succeeded Sir Henry Loch as Patron.

Victorian Scots who held the office of President of the Caledonian Society of Melbourne during the 1890s included Glasgow-born Sir John McIntyre (from 1896 to 1898), who had joined the gold rush as a young man and made a fortune, and the shipping magnate, Sir Malcolm McEacharn (from 1898 to 1901). In 1901, during McEacharn's presidency, the Society played a leading part in the celebrations surrounding the inauguration of the Commonwealth of Australia, welcoming back their former Patron, the Earl of Hopetoun, who had returned to be the country's first Governor-General.

Over the years many Australian Scots were the guests of the Society at its concerts and dinners. One young guest, who sang Scots songs for the members in her youth, was Helen Mitchell (1861-1931), the daughter of a Scots immigrant from Forfar, who later took the professional name of Melba (after the town of her birth), and became famous as one of the world's greatest operatic sopranos. Although her career took her all over the world, Dame Nellie Melba never lost her affection for her home town, and returned to sing for the Society at the height of her fame. A noted speaker at the Society's dinners on several occasions was Andrew Fisher (1862-1928), a coal miner from Crosshouse in Ayrshire, who emigrated to Queensland in 1885. He worked there as a miner, and as a union leader, before entering politics and rising to become Prime Minister of Australia on three occasions.

Sydney members of the New South Wales Scottish Rifles, c.1908. *By permission of Martin J. Buckley, Esq.*

There was an upsurge of activity by Scots and their societies around the turn of the century. In 1885, a volunteer militia force, the New South Wales Scottish Rifles, had been raised, complete with Pipes and Drums, and in 1898 the Victorian Scottish Regiment was established. Scottish sentiment was expressed by the erection of Burns statues — one was unveiled in Melbourne in 1904, and Adelaide and Sydney followed suit within a year. Another development was the launch in Melbourne in 1902 of a monthly journal, *The Scot at Hame an' Abroad*, which continued in existence until 1931. It reported Scottish affairs in Victoria and in the other states, sketched the careers of eminent Scottish-Australians, and published verse and humorous dialect pieces. Allan McNeilage, an emigrant Glaswegian, was a regular contributor of verse, such as the lines written to congratulate the Royal Caledonian Society of Melbourne on its move to new premises in 1923:

> Noo ye have gotten a hoose o' yer ain,
> Hearty good wishes tae send ye I'm fain;
> May ye live lang tae bide here, in peace an' content.
> Wi' nae landlord tae fash ye each week for the rent.

Burns Monument. Melbourne.

Burns monument, Melbourne. *By permission of the Royal Historical Society of Victoria.*

In Sydney, the Highland Society of New South Wales was formed in 1877 through the alliance of a St Andrew's Scottish Benevolent Society and a Caledonian Society, and in 1881 the Royal Caledonian Society of South Australia was born. Five years later, in 1886, the Fremantle Caledonian Society (Western Australia) began its activities, and 1892 saw the establishment of the Brisbane Caledonian Society and Burns Club (Queensland). Thereafter, Scottish societies multiplied in all the states, their fortunes fluctuating as they were influenced by external events, such as the two World Wars.

The music of the pipes has been played in Australia since the earliest days of Scottish settlement, and piping competitions have become an important part of Scottish-Australian life. By 1950, there were over fifty pipe bands in existence. In 1960, when bands were seeking wider contests than their own state championships, an Interstate Conference of their representatives was arranged, and as a result the Australian Federation of Pipe Band Associations was formed. The first Australian Pipe Band Championships, covering all grades, began at Maryborough, Victoria, in 1961.

The Gaelic language spoken by the Highlanders who came to Australia found expression in a periodical first published in Tasmania in 1857, *An Teachdaire Gàidhealach* (The Highland Messenger). This contained news of Australian events as well as Scottish items, but lasted for only nine issues. Gaelic flickered, but did not entirely disappear, for in 1981 the Council for Scottish Gaelic (Comhairle Gàidhlig Albannach) in Sydney decided to revive the periodical as a quarterly. Issue 10 appeared 124 years after Issue 9, and was edited by a Scot from the Isle of Lewis, Mrs Catriona Graham.

At a parade during the annual Easter camp at Liverpool, NSW, in 1906, RSM D. Robertson (left) and QMS J. K. Morice received long service medals. *By permission of Martin J. Buckley, Esq.*

A Scottish Family newly arrived in New South Wales, 1908. *By permission of the New South Wales Government Printing Office.*

SCOTLAND AND AUSTRALIA 1901-1988

PREVIOUS chapters have shown that Scottish exiles contributed significantly to the making of modern Australia. As indicated there, the Scottish impact on Australian development – in social, economic, cultural and political spheres – was quite marked. Before 1900, no fewer than one quarter of a million Scots had braved the tyranny of distance to migrate to Australia, yet given the numerical dominance of the English and the Irish, the overall impact of the Scots was out of proportion to their numbers. However, their impact was probably qualitative rather than quantitative from the start; it was heavily concentrated regionally, especially in New South Wales, Victoria and Queensland; and it was highly dynamic and wide-ranging, covering many spheres of activity from pastoralism to manufacturing. The reply to the query – supposedly from an Irish-Australian around the turn of the century – as to what exactly the Scots had done in Australia was: 'Well, we own it!' This is, perhaps, something of an exaggeration. But what happened after the 1900s? And, nearly a century later, what is the state of the current relationship between Scotland and Australia? Is Australia still a land of exiles? What do Scots and their descendants contribute to the 'Lucky Country', and what has she given back in return? Here, we propose to look briefly at some of the lines of continuity between past and present, as they affect migration of people, capital, culture and politics.

Migration of people, capital and culture – though not necessarily one-way, as we shall see – has remained a major theme in the Scottish-Australian connexion during most of the 20th century. Although the flow of migrants who helped create Australia during the 19th century was much reduced after the 1900s – and, particularly, during the subsequent depression of the 1920s and 1930s – Scots, nevertheless, continued to emigrate in smaller numbers to join longer established settlers. Many of the more politically dynamic Scots were already playing a prominent role in the life of the new Commonwealth of Australia created in 1901.

Even with reduced numbers, the percentage of persons born in Scotland – roughly 2 per cent – continued at much the same level until the onset of the Second World War. Meantime, Australia's population was itself rising:

Table 1: People Born in Scotland as a Percentage of Australia's Population[1]

Year	Scotland %	Total Britain & Ireland %	Total Australia (000s)
1901	2.7	18.0	3,774
1911	2.1	13.3	4,455
1921	2.0	12.4	5,436
1933	2.0	10.8	6,630
1947	1.4	7.2	7,579

1. Table adapted from Table 4.2 (p.94) of David Lucas. *The Welsh, Irish, Scots and English in Australia.* Canberra: Australian Institute of Multicultural Affairs, 1987.

This, and other evidence, suggests that the proportion of Scottish migrants per capita of the home population was high, relative to other parts of Britain and Ireland. Even in 1947, 1.4 per cent of a population of 7.5 million still claimed to be Scots-born. Much the same was true of the post-war

Table 2: Proportion of Scottish Immigrants Entering Australia, 1983-1986[1]

	1983	1984	1985	1986
Total UK	18,620	11,150	12,010	18,722
Scotland	2,540	1,567	1,737	2,941
% Scottish	13.64	14.05	14.46	15.71

Table 3: Scottish Migrants and Funds Arriving in Australia, 1983-1987[1]

	1983[a]	1984	1985	1986	1987
Confirmed arrivals[b]	2,540	1,567	1,737	2,941	738
Persons Visaed	2,362	1,683	2,113	3,251	2,159
Cases Visaed	1,111	900	1,083	1,563	913
Funds[c]	24.70	23.50	33.60	56.50	47.60
Funds/Cases Visaed	22,000	26,000	31,000	36,000	52,000

1. *Source:* Department of Immigration and Ethnic Affairs, Canberra.

2. *Notes:*

(a) The figures for 1983 will be slightly understated because of the carry-over of case work not reported to MPMS.

(b) The number of persons issued with visas in Edinburgh (including a small proportion of persons of non-Scottish origin) confirmed as having arrived during the year specified. Arrivals for 1987 to end of March only.

(c) Funds 'available for transfer' (in A\$ millions).

Source: Department of Immigration and Ethnic Affairs, Canberra.

years, when there was sustained assisted migration from Scotland to Australia throughout the later 1940s and 1950s, and, subsequently, at more modest levels during the 1960s and 1970s. This wave of migrants took much-needed skills to a rapidly developing country with quite specific labour shortages—and, latterly, helped alleviate unemployment at home. One survey undertaken by the Australian Government in 1958 compared the origins of emigrants to Australia with the regional distribution of the population of Britain, and showed that Scotland, with 13.6 per cent of the sampled migrants, had only 10 per cent of the British population. This historical pattern has since been sustained, for during the period 1975 to 1981, the geographical origins of emigrants sampled in the International Passenger Survey again showed that Scotland was one of only two regions (the other being London and the south-east of England) over-represented relative to United Kingdom census data.

In the 1980s, Australia remains a popular destination for Scottish migrants. The Australian Consulate in Edinburgh receives over 2,000 enquiries per month, and, typically, about 10 per cent follow up their interest in migrating to the sun-burnt country. Recent trends in the number of Scottish migrants, and estimates of the capital they take with them to Australia, are summarized in Tables 2 and 3.

While there is a consistent and significant migration of Scots to Australia in recent times, perhaps one of the most remarkable aspects is the extent of capital expatriated with Scots when they migrate. Modern Scottish migrants take with them substantial funds to start their new lives in Australia — an average now of A\$50,000 per head — a fortune by the standard of their relatively impoverished predecessors. Aggregated, Scottish expatriated funds injected an extraordinary A\$56m into the Australian economy in 1986. With the recent collapse of the dollar, Scottish expatriated funds are now even higher per immigrant. Needless to say, the present high level of Scottish investment in Australia through immigration is a continuance of a long tradition of Scottish investment in Australia.

In contemporary Australia itself, as David Lucas has shown, the Scots—like the English, Irish or Welsh—can hardly be identified as 'separate peoples' or 'ethnics', but, nevertheless, those with Scots ancestry perceive themselves as being distinctive. According to one estimate of the ethnic origins of the Australian population, nearly 15 per cent claimed Scottish ancestry in 1947, while in 1978 the figure remained at over 12 per cent. At this later date, five million of Australia's people were thought to be first or second generation Australians, and, of them, over seven per cent were Scottish. Many others felt 'Scottish' to some degree. It is said that one Scottish family in every five has a relative of some kind living in Australia! This further confirms the historical position of the Scots in Australia as a minority in the modern ethnic and cultural mix—but a significant one for all that.

Like most ethnic groups, the Scots in Australia cherish both their origins and their culture. Scottish culture, in its widest sense, flourishes 'Down Under'. Two recent surveys (in 1981 and 1984) by the Department of Immigration and Ethnic Affairs (based on the *Australian Directory of Ethnic Community Organizations*) have shown that of 103 such organizations in 1984, no fewer than 35 were Scottish—and all of these had mainly social and cultural aims of some sort. Other evidence suggests that Scottish societies—invariably in different guises—are much more numerous. One commentator, writing in 1984, thought that Sydney alone had 30 pipe bands, 40 Scottish clubs, and 40 clan societies!

The Scottish Australian Heritage Council was established in 1981 to heighten awareness of the enormous contribution made to the growth and development of Australia by Scots, and by Australians of Scottish descent. Among the Council's aims are the promotion of Gaelic language and literature in Australia, and the raising of funds to establish a Chair of Gaelic Studies at the University of Sydney. The Council also presents annual awards for special contributions to Australia's multicultural heritage, especially in relation to Scottish-Australian activities, which it encourages and publicizes through *The Scottish Australian*

Andrew Fisher. *By permission of James G. Fisher, Esq.*

Sir Robert Menzies. *By permission of Australian Overseas Information Service, London.*

Heritage Council Annual. It also organizes a Sydney Scottish Week each year. The Scottish Australian Heritage Council has played a prominent role in the present arrangements for placing a cairn of stones gathered from different areas of Scotland on an appropriate site—commemorating two hundred years of the Scottish-Australian connexion. Clearly, the aims of the Council work their way through to local societies. For example, the twin objects of the Wollongong Burns

Society are 'to encourage the study of and to stimulate the development of Scottish culture, literature, history, art and music', as well as 'to keep alive the old Scottish tongue, and in particular the works of Robert Burns, the Scottish poet'.

Much Scottish culture in Australia is apparently attractive to others, for the *Canberra Times* reported recently that many of the players in the Canberra Caledonian Pipes and Drums Band had not even a drop of Scots blood in their veins. It seems that 'the lure of the bagpipes can attract any Australian, with or without Scottish connections.... The only things used by the band members which actually hail from Scotland are the bagpipes and the Ancient Campbell tartan!'

During the 20th century, the historical lines of continuity between Scotland and Australia are seen in many walks of life—politics, business, and the media, to name but three. Many Australians of Scots ancestry have played a prominent role in the country's modern politics, both at State and Commonwealth levels. The Commonwealth of Australia was proclaimed in Sydney by the first Governor-General, Lord Hopetoun, on 1 January 1901; while one of the most famous of the early Prime Ministers, Andrew Fisher, was from an Ayrshire mining family. He had previously been a member of the first Labour government in the world, which briefly held power in Queensland during 1899. Scottish blood also flowed in the veins of Australia's longest-serving Prime Minister, the redoubtable Sir Robert Menzies; and, more recently, Malcolm Fraser, descended from a long-established pastoral family, held the same office. In business and the media — two spheres where native Australian genius excels—space allows us to cite only one example. Rupert Murdoch, from relatively modest beginnings, has built a powerful media empire stretching around the globe, embracing newspapers, television stations, and an enormous range of other enterprises — including some in the land of his ancestors.

The example of Rupert Murdoch indicates that the Scottish-Australian relationship is now a much less one-way affair. One of the most significant developments in recent times has been the marked flow of Australian capital into the Scottish economy. At least six Australian companies, including Hume Pipes, and a number of other light engineering companies associated with the oil industry, have subsidiary companies based in Scotland. Australian influence has recently been extended by, for example, the acquisition of the Clydesdale Bank by the National Australia Bank. In addition, the paper manufacturer, J. A. Weir of Kilbagie, has been bought by the Melbourne-based OVS Investment Corporation. An interest in Allied-Lyons, the parent company of the Alloa Brewery Company, has been taken by Bond Corporation. Other interests include the acquisition of the Edinburgh-based New Australia Investment Trust by Mosskirk; the Ailsa shipyard at Troon by Perth Corporation; and Selkirk Holdings' London Broadcasting Company (including Radio Forth) by the Darling Downs Television Company. Australians are even buying back parcels of the old country. In 1987, Mr Iain MacNeacail Scoirebhreac, a retired sheep farmer and Australian-born chief of the Clan McNicol, purchased Ben Chrachaig outside Portree on the Isle of Skye, part of the Clan's traditional territory.

The reverse flow from Australia to Scotland, however, is not confined to capital. Scotland benefits from the presence of a small but extremely active Australian expatriate community. In Edinburgh alone, for example, over a thousand Australians registered a vote at the Australian Consulate in Hanover Street at the last Australian General Election. Drawn from a wide range of occupations, the Australian expatriates are especially prominent in academic life, the arts, and business in Scotland. Indeed, Australians are represented well out of proportion to their population in the professional ranks of Scottish universities – including the current Professor of Scottish Literature in the University of Glasgow. Close connexions exist between Scotland and Australia in the administration of the arts, and Australians contribute significantly to the financial, computing and commercial sectors in Scotland. Until quite recently, an Australian citizen headed the Scottish Law Commission.

Australia's Bicentennial is a cause for celebration in Scotland because of long-standing traditions and feelings linking the two countries. Essentially, these arise from the migration of Scots from their native land in search of new opportunities to join what is now a remarkable ethnic mix of peoples from all over the globe. Historically, the contribution of the Scots to the making of Australia—as Eric Richards has indicated—is both powerful and generally worthy of pride. The continuing tradition of migration of people, skills, capital and culture from Scotland two hundred years after the foundation of Australia is, in one sense, being redressed by a modest reverse flow, which has brought to Scotland the vigour and warmth of the Australian character. These and other qualities will undoubtedly help to maintain the dynamic of the Scottish-Australian relationship in years to come.

CONTRIBUTORS

IAN DONNACHIE is Staff Tutor in History in the Open
University in Scotland.

ADRIAN GRAVES is Lecturer in the Department of History,
University of Edinburgh.

ALEXIA HOWE is Assistant Keeper in the Department
of Printed Books, National Library of Scotland.

ERIC RICHARDS is Professor of History in Flinders
University, South Australia.

SUGGESTIONS FOR FURTHER READING

Australian Dictionary of Biography. Melbourne, 1966–.

The Australian Encyclopaedia. 4th ed. Sydney, 1983.

J. D. Bailey. *A Hundred Years of Pastoral Banking*. Oxford, 1966.

D. W. A. Baker. *Days of Wrath: a Life of John Dunmore Lang*. Melbourne, 1985.

Christina Bewley. *Muir of Huntershill*. Oxford, 1981.

T. F. Bride. *Letters from Victorian Pioneers*. Melbourne, 1898.

Sir Thomas M. Brisbane. *Reminiscences*. Edinburgh, 1860.

K. Buckley and K. Klugman. *The History of Burns, Philp*. Sydney, 1981.

S. J. Butlin. *Foundations of the Australian Monetary System, 1788-1851*. Melbourne, 1953.

R. A. Cage. *The Scots Abroad: Labour, Capital, Enterprise, 1750-1914*. London, 1985.

Alec H. Chisholm. *Scots Wha Hae: History of the Royal Caledonian Society of Melbourne*. Sydney, 1950.

Frank Clune. *The Scottish Martyrs*. Sydney, 1969.

John H. L. Cumpston. *Thomas Mitchell, Surveyor-General and Explorer*. London, 1954.

Peter Cunningham. *Two Years in New South Wales*. London, 1827.

Paul De Serville. *Port Phillip Gentlemen*. Melbourne, 1980.

– *Tubbo: the Great Peter's Run*. Melbourne, 1982.

Gordon Donaldson. *The Scots Overseas*. London, 1966.

First Hundred Years: Scotch College, Melbourne, 1851-1951. Melbourne, 1952.

Kathleen Fitzpatrick. *Australian Explorers*. London, 1958.

William C. Foster. *Sir Thomas Livingston Mitchell and his World, 1792-1855*. Sydney, 1985.

Andrew Dewar Gibb. *Scottish Empire*. London, 1937.

Robert Hughes. *The Fatal Shore*. London, 1987.

Ann-Mari Jordens. *The Stenhouse Circle*. Melbourne, 1979.

James Jupp. *Encyclopaedia of the Australian People*. 1988.

Margaret Kiddle. *Men of Yesterday: a Social History of the Western District of Victoria, 1834-1890*. Melbourne, 1961.

John Dunmore Lang. *Historical and Statistical Account of New South Wales*. London, 1834.

– *Reminiscences of My Life and Times*, ed. by D. N. A. Baker. Melbourne, 1972.

Ida Lee. *Early Explorers in Australia*. London, 1925.

David Lucas. *The Welsh, Irish, Scots and English in Australia*. Canberra, 1987.

Margaret E. Macfarlane. *The Scottish Radicals*. Stevenage, 1981.

I. F. McLaren. *John Dunmore Lang: a Comprehensive Bibliography*. Parkville, Victoria, 1985.

D. S. Macmillan. *The Debtor's War*. Melbourne, 1960.

– *Scotland and Australia, 1788-1850: Emigration, Commerce, and Investment*. Oxford, 1967.

W. G. McMinn. *Allan Cunningham, Botanist and Explorer*. Melbourne, 1970.

Lachlan Macquarie. *Journals of his Tours in New South Wales and Van Diemen's Land, 1810-1822*. Sydney, 1956.

D. J. Mabberley. *Jupiter Botanicus: Robert Brown of the British Museum*. Braunschweig and London, 1985.

Sir Thomas Livingston Mitchell. *Journal of an Expedition into the Interior of Tropical Australia*. London, 1848.

– *Three Expeditions into the Interior of Eastern Australia*. London, 1838.

John Shaw Neilson. *Selected Poems*. North Ryde, New South Wales, 1976.

Oxford History of Australian Literature, ed. by L. Kramer. Melbourne, 1981.

Andrew Barton Paterson. *The Collected Verse of A. B. Paterson*. Sydney, 1946.

Malcolm D. Prentis. *The Scots in Australia: a Study of New South Wales, Victoria, and Queensland, 1788-1900*. Sydney, 1983.

Eric Richards. *A History of the Highland Clearances*. Vol.2: *Emigration, Protest, Reasons*. London, 1985.

– 'Varieties of Scottish Emigration in the 19th Century'. *Historical Studies*, 21 (October 1985).

John Ritchie. *Lachlan Macquarie: a Biography*. Carlton, Victoria, 1986.

Stephen H. Roberts. *The Squatting Age in Australia, 1835-1847*. Melbourne, 1935.

Geoffrey Sherington. *Australia's Immigrants*. Sydney, 1980.

M. J. E. Steven. *Merchant Campbell, 1769-1846: a Study of Colonial Trade*. Melbourne, 1965.

John McDouall Stuart. *Explorations in Australia*, ed. by W. Hardman. London, 1864.

Osmund Thorpe. *Mary McKillop*. London, 1957.

B. Wannan. *The Heather in the South*. Melbourne, 1966.

Jonathan Wantrup. *Australian Rare Books, 1788-1900*. Sydney, 1987.

Don Watson. *Caledonia Australis: Scottish Highlanders on the Frontier of Australia*. Sydney, 1984.

David Lindsay Waugh. *Three Years' Practical Experience of a Settler in New South Wales*. Edinburgh, 1838.

W. B. Withers. *History of Ballarat*. 2nd ed. Ballarat, 1887.

INDEX OF NAMES

(Please note that names of minor significance have been omitted from the Index of Names.)

HMSO publications are available from:

HMSO Bookshops

71 Lothian Road, Edinburgh EH3 9AZ   (031) 228 4181
49 High Holborn, London WC1V 6HB   (01) 211 5656 (Counter service only)
258 Broad Street, Birmingham B1 2HE   (021) 643 3740
Southey House, 33 Wine Street, Bristol BS1 2BQ   (0272) 24306/24307
9-21 Princess Street, Manchester M60 8AS   (061) 834 7201
80 Chichester Street, Belfast BT1 4JY   (0232) 234488

HMSO Publications Centre

(Mail and telephone orders only)
PO Box 276, London SW8 5DT
Telephone orders (01) 622 3316
General enquiries (01) 211 5656

HMSO's Accredited Agents

(see Yellow Pages)

And through good booksellers

Printed in Scotland for HMSO CC 42080 50c 6/88 HF 4748